WRITERS REPUBLIC

Five More
Minutes

Deanna Roberto

WRITERS REPUBLIC L.L.C.
515 Summit Ave. Unit R1
Union City, NJ 07087, USA

Website: *www.writersrepublic.com*
Hotline: *1-877-656-6838*
Email: *info@writersrepublic.com*

Ordering Information:
Quantity sales. Special discounts are available on quantity purchases by corporations, associations, and others. For details, contact the publisher at the address above.

Library of Congress Control Number: 2021935887
ISBN-13:   978-1-63728-406-3   [Paperback Edition]
                  978-1-63728-407-0   [Digital Edition]

Rev. date: 08/10/2021

To God, who gave Alexa the most beautiful and joyous 20 years of life on this Earth. Some don't get to spend that much time or even have the opportunity to live everyday like it's their last. I'm so grateful to confidently say that Alexa left this world with some of the most beautiful memories that one could possibly imagine. Life always felt like a dream for her. The people around her surely felt the same way. That was simply due to her smile that lit up each and every room she walked into.

To Mom and Dad who provided Alexa and I with the world. From tenderness and attention to the shoes under our feet and the roof over our head. We are and will forever be beyond thankful to have such hardworking and loving parents that showed us what life is like to make something out of love.

To Grandma, I am sure you and Lex are partying it up and watching down on each and every person who was apart of this journey then and who are following along now. Grandma, there is no bigger inspiration in this world for me, than you. You have taught me absolutely everything I know and I am the person I am today because of you. I can say that with my head held high and the feeling of you always in my heart. I hope I make you proud each and every day as I continue this life.

To Jaime, I'm sure you are up there as well wishing you could have done something to stop Alexa's progression. I hope you both are having the time of your lives watching the Giants play on a flat screen TV.

To Jerry, I am just as positive that God called you home so early because both you and Alexa missed each others hugs. Since the day we met you, you treated us like your own. You inspire me each and every day. Every time I take a photo, I think of you guiding me in my interest in photography. The world was a better place with you in it but now we're here trying to fill your shoes and those big belly laughs each and everyday. I gotta say, no one does it like you!

To everyone that went on this rollercoaster with Alexa:

Grandpa, Nanny
Soraya, Val, Dayanara, Vanessa, Omar, Christopher, Nicholas, Paul, The Landolfi Family, The Sciove Family, The Tobar Family, The Ally Family, The Rodriguez Family,

The Stolfa Family, The Wrzec Family, The Tamburillo Family,
The Kessel Family, The Halpin Family, The Spallino Family, The Luke
Family
The Amato Family, The Ciorciari Family, The Ruggiero Family, The
Cerverizzo Family,
Our family at St. Mel's Catholic Academy, The Mary Louis Academy,
Maritime College

"She was just an angel that needed to be sent home."

Nicholas Votta

1. OHANA

My sister Alexa was born on March 16, 1998 to two loving and deserving parents, Lou and Sandra. She was born in St. Johns Hospital and was immediately loved and cared for by just about everyone that came in contact with her. I'd like to say that was everyone's reaction to me when I was born a couple years later but, who knows. We were both blessed when we were born into such an elaborate group of family and friends. Pay attention and try not to get too confused. On my moms side, she is one of five. It's our mom Sandra, aunts Soraya (Yaya), Dayanara (Dayday) and Vanessa (Sesa) and our Uncle Jaime. Their parents are Beatrice and Jaime, our Grandma and Grandpa Nino. My dad on the other hand, is an only child. His parents Diane and Nick are our Grandma and Grandpa Roberto. We also had a literal God sent in our family, our Great Aunt (grandpa Roberto's sister) Lucy who we call Nanny. Alexa and I also have incredible Godparents. We shared in our Uncle Joe's love and branched off to separate incredible godmothers; her's being Sesa and mine being my Aunt Val. My Aunt Val is Soraya's best friend and she's been apart of our family since before either of us were born. It's safe to say, she's just about as blood related and wild as the rest of us. All of our dads 'brothers' that we consider our Uncles are the best extended family anyone could ever ask for. If that's not enough, with them came even more aunts and cousins, an ongoing and continuously growing family. Alexa and I were lucky enough to not only grow up with these incredible people and love them as much as they love us, but we were also able to rewatch ourselves grow up when Vanessa and her husband, our uncle Omar, had both of our 'little bros', Chris and Nicky. The only difference was that they were a few years younger, but that didn't stop us from wrestling and constantly ganging up on each other like all siblings would. If you were to see them now, between their height and their protective manner, you would think they're *our* over protective older brothers. But trust me, we were once taller than both of them…and I promise we weren't on our tippy toes. It's pretty neat to know that someone has your back as much as they constantly have ours. Its also pretty cool to know that a majority of these people have been there for the both of us since birth and continued to stick by us as individuals each and every day, no matter how annoying we both grew up to be. Even though family could be difficult sometimes, and trust me, I know we've all been there, what a genuine blessing it truly is to have such an astounding group of people in our lives that we are fortunate enough to call our family, our Ohana.

2. GRANDPARENTS, SCHOOL, ALEXA, OH MY

When Alexa and I were growing up, a majority of our memories consisted of traveling back and forth from our Grandma Roberto's house to our Grandma Nino's party store. We had the privilege of spending our childhood years growing up and learning from both of them. Having such a strong relationship with both sets of grandparents was truly a blessing. However, in August of 2004, our Grandpa Nino passed away from a heart attack. The following year, in September of 2005, our Grandma Nino passed from ovarian cancer. Both were extreme losses to not only us but to our entire family as a whole. It's never easy loosing a loved one but letting go of two people, one after the other is even more difficult. Although I don't personally remember either of them much, one thing I do remember about my Grandma Nino specifically was spending time at her party store in Corona with Lex.

Both sets of our grandparents helped raise my sister and I due to our parents working full time. They agreed to have us for certain days out of the week. When my Grandma Nino had us, we spent our days at her store. Alexa, being three years older than me, has a much better memory of both our Grandma and Grandpa Nino. However, this one specific recollection of my Grandma Nino is one that will remain with me forever.

Every time we were at her store, I had a special spot all to myself, the countertop holding a bottle full of Frunas, my favorite Spanish candy. She would always make it a point to buy the blue raspberry ones, which were my absolute favorite. She would constantly hide them in the bottom of the container so that I would have to dig my little hands to the base to search for them. It was like a real life version of Where's Waldo but instead of looking for a little stripe shirted man I was looking for my damn raspberry candy. I would stuff my two year old hands in as quick as possible so Lex didn't get to them first; you bet your ass I found them before she did.

After they had both passed away, our Grandma and Grandpa Roberto took care of us full time alongside Nanny. They were the people that I remembered the most during my childhood, and with that being said, I had the absolute best childhood one could possibly wish for. They were and will forever be the greatest people that have been in my life. They did everything for the both of us... literally. When Alexa was beginning school, my parents and my grandma decided that she would attend St. Mels School which was the area zones private Catholic school in Whitestone, where my grandparents lived. With that, when September rolled around and Alexa began school, our brutal everyday routine for the next 12 years started; though honestly, I wouldn't of wanted it any other way. Confused? A lot of people are when I tell them I live in two places at once, so let me break it down for you. First, we would wake up at 6. When I say 'wake up' I mean the yelling to wake us up would begin at 6. This vocal scene included our mom continuously shouting at us to wake up because "grandpa is outside". This then led to the constant banging of her rings on our bedroom door and threatening to pour water on us. It concluded by us finally rolling out of bed due to pure annoyance. If you think this only went on when we were young, you're definitely in the wrong. This routine occurred everyday until Alexa got her license when she was 19. Okay, now back to the routine. After our lazy asses rolled out of bed, we would rush to get ready because they were going to be there by 6:30 and grandma was not one that enjoyed waiting, simply because the rest of the 'daily routine' would be thrown off. Grandpa on the other hand would stay there all day and wait and somehow make it to each place in a timely manor. I swear he deserved the perfect attendance award each year more than Lex and I did.

About three phone calls and an angry grandma later, Alexa and I would finally leave our home in Jackson Heights and hop into Grandpas renowned gray van. We would get to Whitestone at around 7 and rush to have breakfast, either cereal, waffles or pancakes. Then, Lex would get her school uniform on, slip on her cute little Disney backpack, and be on her way. As per usual, Alexa always felt the need to be early to school, even though it was only Pre-K. God forbid she missed playing with Sunny the stuffed animal before anyone else and the rest of the day was just completely out the window. My grandpa would drive Alexa and my grandma to school while I stayed home with Nanny. While they were rushing for no apparent reason, Nanny and I were having a grand ole time doing Scooby Doo mad libs on the couch after breakfast. That is and will always be one of my favorite memories of us because we would both laugh uncontrollably at the dumb stuff a 4 year old would make up.

After the grey van pulled up and both my grandparents were home, my grandma booked it to the couch so we could have some grammy/granddaughter time. We watched TV all the way until 12:30 when Lex had to be picked up. From The Big Comfy Couch to The Doodlebops; the hours from 9 until 12:30 was me, grandma, and a can of Pringles, sitting on the couch binge watching PBS Kids. Our alarm clock as to when we had to begin our journey to St. Mel's was when we heard the Lazy Town theme song. Once we heard it for the second time, we knew we had to hit the sidewalks of Whitestone to go pick up my sister.

Taking the walk with my grandma was always an adventure. She would hold my hand all the way there and back which made my little self feel all warm and fuzzy inside. We would walk all of 8 blocks to get to St. Mels to pick up Lex and then walk the same route back home. The best part of picking her up was stopping by the house with the red honeysuckle berry bush. Each time we walked by it we would pick as many berries as could fit in our little hands and stomp on them as walked home, watching out light up sneakers have a party with each hard step. We were definitely sister goals.

Once we got home, our grandmas favorite time of the day would begin. No, it was not spending time with the both of us, although I hope that was at least on the top 3 behind cooking and going to KeyFood and Target. It was now soap opera time! From 1pm until 4pm we watched three different soaps together. Lex and I both watched alongside grams while she helped us with our homework. If that wasn't balancing enough things at once, she also got up during each commercial to finish making dinner. A master at multitasking if I do say so myself.

God blessed our family with the ability to not only have a Sunday dinner together, but have one each and every night. Honestly, that was Lex and I's favorite part of our childhood. Alexa's mainly because grandma would make her 'special pasta' which consisted of any pasta with shredded mozzarella on top. If that wasn't enough, she also had it *all* to herself. For me, it was because grammy would literally make anything and everything I wanted; also known as dinosaur chicken nuggets, french fries and mozzarella sticks. If you can't clearly tell, our Grandma was a real life superhero.

Once my dad got out of work he would come straight to grandmas house for dinner and my mom would do the same. No one ever missed dinner and if you did, you better have a damn good reason to back your absence up. Dinner was our family moment, to sit and appreciate each other while also having an exquisite home cooked meal brought to you by none other than my grandma. I kid you not, she was the absolute best cook and I'm not just saying that because we're related, literally everyone agreed. People that were walking their dogs on our block would knock on the door and poke their heads in to tell her that they could smell the amazing aromas outside. So, you can only imagine how each and every one of our dinners were; five star meals with enough to feed the whole freaking block.

After dinner was over, we all would watch some of our favorite TV shows together. Ya know, Survivor on this day and The Amazing Race on that day with a little bit of Dancing with the Stars in the middle. It was all written down in the TV guide that my grandma brought home each and every week. When the festivities were over, we would all go home for the night. Lex and I would "go to sleep" at 11…well, I mean at least the attempt was there. We would get a little sidetracked laughing at the complete bullshit stories we made up during our 'pajama time'. With that, our routine would start up again at 6 am.

When I started going to St. Mel's the routine stayed the same but the connection I had with my sister was very different. I guess the older I got, the more attached to her I became. I basically wanted to walk in her shadow each and every second I could. Going to the same school as her definitely allowed me to do so with ease; even though she hated having a mini her following her every move. Alexa would constantly tell me to do my own thing and leave her alone but I clearly didn't listen very well. So… basically not much changed since then.

When grandma and grandpa dropped us both off in the morning, Alexa would go to her 2nd grade classroom while I started down the hall to my kindergarten classroom. However I would take a sharp left and follow

Lex down to her room because, 'I didn't want to be alone'. I was obviously doing it for her sake. I was clearly making sure she was okay without me, duh. Eventually I would be walked to my own classroom down the hall in which I would spend the entire day sitting on the floor waiting for Alexa to pass by. I sat criss cross applesauce, starring out the window on the left of the door as I waited. She would only pass by my classroom door once a week when her class went to the gym, though I sat there each and every day and continued to wait...just incase. In case of what? I don't really know, but ya know, just in case. Boy was I lame.

3. TMLA, THE MARY LOUIS ACADEMY, (T)HE (M)EMORIES (L)AST, (A)LWAYS

In 2012 Alexa graduated St. Mels School and was fortunate enough to not only get accepted, but also attend the high school that was her first choice, The Mary Louis Academy. In 2015 when I graduated, you could probably imagine where I was going, following Lex straight to TMLA. When Alexa first got to TMLA, it was very obvious that it was *the* place for her. She excelled not only academically but was able to step out of her personal comfort zone. Before then, she always kept to herself and was very quiet. At Mary Louis she felt comfortable enough to express herself. With the constant support of the powerful woman and people around her, this 'new place' allowed her to really shine. In addition, all of the influential people that she came in contact with throughout those 4 years, she also found her best friend very early into her high school career, Isabella Spallino.

Isabella and Alexa found each other at the start of their freshwoman year but they weren't always attached by the hip. When they first met, Bella was scared of Lex and thought that she was going to bully her. However, a few weeks later, through a proper introduction and many classes and lunches spent together, they became nothing short of "future bridesmaids".

They expanded their group shortly after and became best friends with Caitlin Kessel and Kailey Halpin. From my point of view, it was my dream to find friends like them. When Alexa felt at her lowest, especially when our dad had open heart surgery that year, they supported and comforted not only her but me as well. All of their qualities and quirks were what I wanted to find in my own friends. So, in 2015 when I began at TMLA, I was on a mission to do the same. I wanted to make friendships that would last a lifetime. I wanted to find my future bridesmaids, just like Lex did.

Through trial and error I was able to find incredible friends throughout my years there. My best friend Carly who has taught me what real friendship is. Bella, who accepted and encouraged me to be myself in every situation possible, besides the fact that we are literally twins in so many ways. Isabelle, Daniella, Layla, Briana, Emily, Sarina, Lucia and many more women that had become my friends throughout my years there and have accepted me for who I am and nothing less, who have had my back and been there for me even when we don't always agree. Although we don't see each other or talk everyday, whenever we are together, we pick up right where we left off. What a genuine blessing that is to have found friends like that. Although finding those gems didn't come easy for me, I believe I found my bridesmaids and I would say if TMLA gave us both anything besides an education, it was a lifelong family. Lex and I both honestly couldn't of asked for anything more.

My favorite year at Mary Louis was my freshwoman year because…. yep you guessed it, my sister was there. She showed me the ropes of the 'high school life' at TMLA and I genuinely wouldn't of wanted to learn from anyone else. She introduced me to so many incredible people that I continue to keep in contact with and look up too each and every day. From individuals such as Mrs. Flynn, Mr. Lewinger, Mrs. Rodgers, Mrs. Alberici, Mrs. Russo, Mr. McCarthy, and so many more of those influential teachers that got her through some of her most difficult days at school. I of course, then became dependent on those teachers to help me function throughout each and every day, from beginning to end.

Alexa is the smartest person I know and I will forever be extremely jealous of her huge brain filled with Math, Science, and so much more. However, I can't relate. I can't do any of that smart people stuff. I stick to Art, Sports, and English because genuinely, that's all I can manage. Lex's favorite class during her senior year was Forensics Science, so when I lost my beloved TMLA planner (my baby), I knew exactly who to put on the case. However, the first thing I had to do was find the investigator, so I ran downstairs to the locker room to check her schedule that she kept taped to the inside. My smart ass didn't know how to unlock a lock before attending TMLA so thankfully she taught me by using her lock, so I knew the combo. Though, I would've been shit out of luck if I didn't remember it.

Once I figured out what class she was in, I ran upstairs and tried to wave her down through the tiny window without getting her into trouble. With no luck there, I ran back up to Mrs. Russo's class which is where I was *supposed* to be. Within minutes Lex came knocking on her door to see what the problem was. When Mrs. Russo saw Alexa's smiling face and turned around to see my tearful eyes, she excused herself and I from class and stepped outside with us to discuss what was wrong. While Lex explained the situation, Mrs. Russo rolled her eyes and laughed at us as I began crying into her shoulder, weeping about the loss of my beloved planner. She knew I had to go on this mission. Now, if that doesn't prove that us Roberto's cry about literally everything, than I don't know what does. Also, if you were not fortunate enough to of had this kind of relationship with a teacher, I apologize, you really missed out. If you are never able to encounter someone like Mrs. Russo, I also apologize. You should probably try to find someone as loving, caring, humble, passionate and motherly as her. If not, swing by TMLA and tell her I sent you.

Well anyway, Lex and I were on the hunt for my planner, and after a few extremely long classes without my literal child, my planner was found and you best believe I never let that thing out of my sight again. What an intriguing memory, I know. But honestly, stupid stuff like that really shows how much my sister was there for me through literally *everything*. Even when things seemed minor, she had my back and helped me solve my seemingly pointless problem. So yeah, TMLA gave me best friends and bridesmaids, but my forever friend and my maid of honor was one that I had the opportunity to call my sister.

When Alexa graduated high school, I was officially on my own in this semi adult life because her real adult life was about to begin. Yep, I'm talking about college. Alexa attended Maritime College in which she majored in Marine Biology and minored in Marine Environmental Science. So basically, she wanted to swim with the dolphins. I was all for her going to Maritime because not only was the school on the freakin water with an insanely beautiful view, but it was also 85% male and 15% female IN UNIFORM. So lets be real, I was all for that :)

However, because I know my sister like an open book, a new school meant learning new buildings, making new friends, and having new schedules. College meant growing up and looking towards the future.

None of which Lex was ready for and none of which I was ready to let happen. I didn't want to stop hanging out and I wanted to continue being the weirdos we've always been; if that was the result of her growing up, I for one didn't want it. When Lex would come home late at night because she was studying for finals and midterms, I was not super excited about the sole hour of visitation I received, followed by her knocking out on the couch or in bed, whatever was closer. That lasted days, sometimes even weeks. However the only comfort I acquired about her being at school all the time was the fact that she was experiencing her new adult life with her best friend, (that she met at Maritime) Geresa. A crazy loving bestie that had the same passion for school and had the same major as Lex. Not only was she an incredible friend to Lex but she became a second sister to me. This eventually allowed us both to meet her astounding family who quickly became our family as well, which we were practically adopted into in no time. Mom and Dad (Theresa and Gerry Luke), were our home away from home. Whenever we would go over, we were greeted by warm hugs from dad and kisses from mom. If that wasn't 'home-y' enough, she had siblings! Yes, there was more where that love came from! Dale and Fabian who just as quickly became our big brothers and Liani who became my soul sister and Lex's second little sis. Geresa and Alexa were the best friends that you and your bestie aspired to be. Not only were they both inanely smart and talented, they had the greatest personalities and brought out the best in each other. What more could two ask for? Let me be the first to tell you that Alexa was the absolute best at making friends, but she was even better at making them family and that was genuinely my favorite part of each of the genuine friendships that she made throughout her life. Every 'friend' and their families that I have mentioned thus far have become apart of OUR family. She was blessed with the best people and what an ongoing bliss that was to continue to extend our family.

However, my favorite part about Alexa going to college was that she *finally* learned how to drive. Besides driving to school each morning at 7am to get a 'close parking spot' when she had a 10am class, she also became my personal Uber driver. However she thoroughly enjoyed driving, so it was kind of a win win for both of us, right? Every day that she had classes and didn't need to stay after school to study or work, she would pick me up from school and we would go on an after school date. Those were some of my favorite days. We would get pizza together, go to Applebees or grab lunch at Christinas and go home to exchange whatever gossip we had for the day and listen to each other about life, friends, or problems. Whatever our conversations were about, we would both always share our critical, but loving, wise words of wisdom to each other.

Lex and I really needed some of those wise words from the beginning to the middle of 2016. Why? Because our caretaker, our walking buddy, our best friend, got sick. Our grandma got sick in 2016 and was diagnosed with ALS halfway throughout the year. I for one, was not familiar with the disease but Lord knows I wish I could never be exposed to it again. ALS is a progressive disease in which over time, functions and organs of the body begin to deteriorate and fail. That is exactly what happened to my grandma within a year, and what a traumatic year that turned out to be.

My grandpa and I were the two main people that took care of her due to my parents working full time and Alexa studying and working at Maritime. So it was my grandpa and I till the very end, and honestly if we had the opportunity to do it all again, we would do it in a heartbeat.

When she was officially diagnosed with ALS, we had a nursing team, therapists, and aids that would care for her and help her in hope to slow down the process as much as possible. Although there is no cure, they would attempt to benefit her movements and abilities as they began to gradually decrease. Because I was going to school in the mornings until mid afternoon, I would set up the aid scheduling for the times when I wasn't present. When I came back home they would leave and I would be able to care for her for the rest of the day. I would set up the nursing and therapy appointments for later in the day so that I could watch what they were doing and continue the exercising on the days they weren't present. I would do anything to slow down this disgusting developing disease.

Everyday it was something new. One day everything seemed fine and the next she lost the mobility in her hands. The following week her legs began to become sore and weak. The next few months she had little to no movement in her legs at all. However, grandpa and I kept on caring for her. From bringing her ice pops because she had a dry mouth to sitting her up and attempting leg therapy each day. Boy, we would do anything to turn back time to the better days. But unfortunately, this disease was kicking my ass as much as my grandma wanted to kick *it* in the ass. Soon after her limbs became immobile, her voice started to fade and her throat began closing. Even then, one of my grandma's favorite therapists would not give up on her. She would do therapy with her in the kitchen so she could continue teaching me how to cook, from sauce to chili and so much more, she never stopped anything. To be completely honest, she didn't stop until it stopped her.

The day was June 28, 2017 when I went to my grandma's house like any other day. When I walked through the front door, I called for my grandpa to see where he was, but everything and everyone was silent. I walked towards the bedroom and saw him sitting next to my grandma's hospital bed, holding her hand with his head down. My grandma didn't even look like herself, and to tell you my heart sank to the floor was an understatement. Although she wasn't doing well the previous night, within the last 12 hours she had gotten extremely worse. I left them both in the back together and went into the living room to call everyone. I knew this would be it, her last few hours in this world and I wanted to make sure that everyone was able to say their goodbyes. I called my dad first, who within the minute he picked up the phone. My sister was next and within a blink of an eye she was present. My mom took a cab from home. Vanessa, Chris and Nicky practically flew here and the same goes for Soraya, Dayanara and my Aunt Val. My grandma had done so much and been such a role model for everyone in our family that nobody even hesitated when I called and told them to come to her house to show their love. With the grace of God everyone was able to pay their respects to such an incredible life taken so soon. At 10:56 pm, I had, we had, Heaven had, gained a guardian angel.

This was the first time I was loosing someone so close to me. I never experienced a pain like that until then, and I truly wish I never had to experience it again. I couldn't understand why and how everything happened so quickly. There was genuinely no time to process anything. I tried to think of all the things I had done wrong and figured maybe if I tried harder with PT or stressed how important in was to get up every day that she could of potentially had a few more days. I couldn't and will probably never understand why diseases exist. Is it so people understand heartbreak? So people could experience death in one of the worst ways possible? I cannot comprehend any of it. I believed and still do believe that my grandma taught me and I'm sure the rest of my family, everything that there is to learn in this world except how to continue life in this crazy place without her to guide us…

4. GOING TO THE BIG APPLE FOR A BIG DAY

November 11, 2017 started off like any other day, Alexa and I were going on another adventure. This time, we were celebrating Geresa's 19th birthday. The plan was to meet up at G's house and travel into the city together to explore and have dinner at her favorite restaurant; and that's exactly how the idea of the day progressed. Alexa and I drove to her house with their other friend Tyler, and soon enough, we all were ready to head out to the streets of Brooklyn to catch the next train into Manhattan.

While Alexa, Tyler, and I played follow the leader with Geresa and Liani, we eventually made it to the train station. We huddled around each other to suppress the numbness in our hands and feet due to the frigid cold November day. Of course Alexa wasn't cold though, she wore a lightweight North face jacket and was "just fine". I didn't know being 'just fine' came with slight shive but let's go with that. After our 'lack of warmth huddle' made it clear to everyone in Brooklyn that the five people getting on the train were clearly deranged, we started down the stairs so Alexa and I (the worst New Yorkers ever) could get metro cards. Who knew the walk down the train station stairs would be where this life altering twist began, where Alexa's life would be shifted forever, where eventually all of our hearts would be shattered.

While I was walking down the stairs towards the metro card vending machines, I felt someone pulling at my jacket from behind me. I knew it was Alexa tugging at me so I didn't bother to turn around. I figured her clumsy ass tripped on the stairs and her clean freak self didn't want to touch the railing. Though when she did it again, I turned right around and proceeded to incite some of my natural attitude by saying, "Okay? What the hell". After looking up at her pale face, I realized she wasn't grabbing onto me to annoy me or to steady her Bambi ass self, there was something clearly wrong. Her response as everyone could probably imagine was,

"Nothing, I'm fine". She seemed to always be *just fine*…until she wasn't.

I know my sister like the back of my damn hand. No matter how much she insists that I don't, I promise you, I do. While we do have a sister connection, it's also due to the fact that if she's not either smiling, being sarcastic, or annoying me, she's either sad, upset, or sick. Her emotions don't have much of a range after that.

After a train ride filled with humor and jokes that only the five of us will ever understand along with timeless reminiscing about God knows what, we finally made it into Manhattan. We walked down the long New York City blocks towards Times Square and all was well…so far. We all strutted down the streets with power, pride and hearts full of love and celebration, ready to have a fun filled night, or at least that was the primary intention. As we were making our way towards the heart of the city, Alexa yet again started holding onto me. Again, I asked her the same question and I figured I was going to receive the same response, but this time I was wrong. Instead of her usual "I'm good" bullshit, she told me she was feeling really dizzy. My hypochondriac self immediately thought of 5 million things but instead of expressing them and scaring her (but mostly me), I reacted by asking her if she wanted to go home and cut the night short.

However, for anyone that knows Alexa, they know that she was always there for her family and friends and so she said,

"Nope, we're celebrating G's birthday. I'm fine". (see, I knew that 'I'm fine' was coming at some point). With that, we continued walking.

Finally, we made it to Times Square. We took photos on the famous 'Red Steps' and all collectively watched Geresa fall in potentially the most populated area in the city over her own two feet. She had to fall at least once to make it a successful night. We all responded with nothing but laughter as we watched her struggle to get up. If thats not true friendship/sisterhood, I don't know what is.

Our journey continued into Central Park where we decided to scale giant rocks at 10 pm. Yes, on this date, we decided to become professional rock climbers. Three falls later, two from…yep you guessed it, Geresa, and one from me trying to get Alexa to climb up with us, we finally made it to the top of what seemed like the tallest rock in the park. In reality we were about five feet off the ground and to our surprise, us girls were just really short.

Being all together at Central Park made us feel like we were on top of the world…or on top of a rock, but you get the point. We made it to G's favorite restaurant and had dinner before our excursion back home. Alexa and I drove from Brooklyn back to Queens and not much was said about the whole being dizzy situation. It was more of a casual karaoke ride home, as per our usual.

5. THE SUPER BOWL 'HEARD ROUND THE WORLD'

The common theme of this real life story seems to be that life plans don't always go as perceived. No matter how much you plan for the future, those plans could be condensed at any second. Moral of the story, live in the moment. Plan for today because a casual calm Friday evening turned out to be the epitome of a rollercoaster ride.

A few days after G's celebration, Lex and I took a road trip to Sesa's house in NJ for the weekend to watch the boys' final game of their football season, their Super Bowl game. Lex picked me up at grandmas house after she finished class and we loaded up her car. She had her one book bag while I had my six duffel bags filled with clothes for about every season. Once we hit the road, it was sister sister time, my favorite! That meant the music was loud, the windows were down and we were singing like nobody was watching. It also included a bit of boy talk and drama, of course. All of New York could hear us belting country music and Disney classics as we made our way onto the expressway. Halfway through the ride to NJ, we got stuck in traffic. As we stood stationary for a while, Lex and I managed to find something to fight about. Though this time, it was about something my overprotective ass took extremely serious.

Although it was October, it was an unusually hot fall Friday, so Alexa decided to take off her hoodie in the middle of driving. Thank goodness we were practically sitting still behind what felt like miles of traffic. As I assisted in pulling the hoodie off from over her head, I happened to catch a glimpse of her arm while tugging at the sleeves. I don't even think anyone could miss what I was looking at. I was staring at huge bruises that were covering a majority of her forearm. The first words that came out of my mouth were, "what the fuck is that". Lex never worried about herself as one could clearly already tell. She often times found the best and did the

19

most for people on such a daily basis that subconsciously she would allow people to "walk over her". With me, that didn't sit very well. I can read people extremely well and as much as I want to see the best in others, I know that often times people will abuse kindness. I knew when someone was taking advantage of me and that shit stopped at the door, but for Alexa, it was a bit harder for her to judge just because of the kind person she was. Her response to my aggressive question was that she simply walked into a wall and of course, she was "fine".

"It's was just a bruise, it'll go away".

I responded with a casual attitude based eye roll and left the conversation open, in hope she decided to tell me the truth. I wasn't so sure if this big ass wall was going to grow arms and bruise her again.

A couple sighs and a few quiet moments later, I looked over at Lex and saw she was crying. I wasn't sure what she was crying about because all I was trying to do was look out for her, but I figured I was maybe *too* aggressive when asking. Though what did she expect me to say, nothing? Couldn't be me. I immediately apologized if I truly upset her in which she responded with a head nod while she grasped at the left side of her face. I genuinely didn't think much of it because in my family it's insanely common to cry over just about everything, so I wasn't really surprised by the dramatic emotion aspect. I was more upset with the fact that she was crying over something I said… or so that's what I thought. A couple minutes later, Lex muttered a few words. I couldn't make out much of what she was saying or trying to say. All I got was that her mouth was hurting. I didn't know what to do because we were in a car and I was not a dentist, so I assured her that Sesa would be able to do something as soon as we got there. I hoped her dental experience background and mom skills would come in handy here. Basically, I just hoped to get out of damn traffic and do something to stop the pain so she would stop crying.

Thankfully within the hour, we finally made it to NJ. We hopped out and left the bags in the car as I rushed to open the front door. As I turned the key, Lex pushed open the door and beelined for the stairs. I stayed downstairs on the couch and waited for everyone to come home. In no time, both Chris and Nicky flung open the door with Sesa traveling behind. They all had the utmost confusion on their face because we were supposed to be surprising them by visiting for the first time with Lex driving to NJ, but in reality, they were about to get the surprise. Once they saw me, they all ran over for hugs and kisses. However, I cut our little celebration short because I practically tossed Sesa up the stair so she could help Lex. As she ran up the stairs, I followed. We burst through the bedroom door and saw her lying face down, sobbing through the sheets and pillows. When she heard the door open, she sat up and opened her mouth, ready to be fixed so the pain could go away. With tears in both of their eyes, Sesa looked for the problem, which seemed to be a bit more problematic than expected. The pain was coming from her wisdom teeth and the fact that they were tremendously impacted and needed to get pulled... like, yesterday.

"How did you not feel this until now? It's been hurting you for a while, right?"

The more words that were spoke, the more tears that streamed down Alexa's face. She finally decided to shut up and get the medicine put on her tooth so Lex could stop the sweating from her eyes. As I presumed, Sesa was there to save the day, thank God, cause there were no other options.

The following night was the boys' Super Bowl game. Our favorite part of coming to see their games was getting them hype before they ran onto the field. That afternoon, we pumped them up by blasting their favorite songs and jamming out together while they got their gear on. After that, the two animals ran onto the field with a fire under their ass to meet up with their team while we, the semi normal ones, casually walked. Lex and I loved watching them play together and kick ass as a team but we also kept our eyes peeled for our *three* boys, Chris, Nicky and their best friend Devin. When we approached the field, we walked up the ramp onto the bleachers and looked around for the one and only, the Burgos family. Jogging up the bleacher stairs, we sat next to them and caught up about life, like usual. Devin's mom, Caren, and I were trying to spot all of our children practicing on the opposite field while Alexa and Joey, Devin's dad, were attempting to explain to Sesa a play that was currently being called for the Pee-Wee's game that was just about finishing up.

As Chris and Nicky were progressively getting older, Lex and I realized that we couldn't stop the process so instead of not accepting that they couldn't be small forever, we decided to talk to them about the ins and outs of life. We would always talk about the importance of true friendship.

They lived in a small town and went to school with the same people even after switching schools as they moved up in grades. We made it a point to educate them on the difference between acquaintances, friends and a best friend/friends. Let's be real, finding someone special that you consider a best friend is tricky, but hey, they obviously learned from the best… Alexa, so I wasn't as worried. When we first met Devin (and his family), we were over the moon about them finally listening to something we said. My first impression of the Burgos family was that they were the kind of people that you wanted to be around all the time.

Even though I know Caren is reading this and saying, "really? Are you sure about that?", I promise you it's the truth.

Now, after getting to know them all better over time, I can confidently say that all I initially thought of them is 100% true. They are incredible people and an overall amazing family. They are all extremely hardworking, intelligent and humble individuals. With that being said, Lex and I already knew that he was someone we hoped both Chris and Nicky would stay around, and we freakin prayed that Devin felt the same. As cliche as it sounds, a super important lesson to learn at a young age is who is going to be there for you and stick by your side through ups and downs. To this day, they are all best friends and I am certain that Lex is as happy as I am to know that they both have another brother that will always have their backs as much as they have his.

Sitting at Rutherford's Tryon field and watching the Bulldogs play as a team for their big game is as incredible and massive as it sounds. The adrenaline on the field matches the adrenaline in the stands. All was going well until it started to torrential downpour towards the end of the game. The Bulldogs were up by a few points and the rain didn't stop anyone from screaming "who let the dogs out" after each touchdown, except Alexa. While she tried to stay upbeat with everyone else, there were a few moments where I would look at her and see pain written cross her face. However, there isn't a thing that she wouldn't do for those boys so she tried her best to masque it. That night, the Rutherford Bulldogs took home the Super Bowl trophy for their town and their team. The celebrations were going to continue at the bonfire afterparty with the entire team, cheerleaders, coaches and everyones families.

After the game was over we all walked home to change out of our soaking wet clothes and warm up before heading back to the field for the bonfire. Lex told me on the walk home that she wasn't feeling to good and that she thinks that she may have caught a draft from being cold for so long. I wanted to respond with, "Maybe you wouldn't of been so cold if you would've worn a jacket" but I decided to swallow my attitude this time. She was telling me that she thinks that the medicine was wearing off because the pain was coming back so I told her to stay home instead of going back out so she could rest. She responded with a head shake no. Does anyone else see a common theme here… stubbornness maybe? I think it runs in the family.

She toughed it out a few hours at the bonfire before she couldn't handle much more 'smiling through the pain'. She asked Sesa for the keys and we walked home together so everyone else could continue enjoying the Super Bowl festivities. We didn't say much on the walk home because I knew she was in too much pain to talk and I didn't want to bother her even more.

As we walked in the door she headed straight for the couch and looked up at me with sad eyes and said, "I'm craving a fruit punch from Burger King."

"What the hell is so special about the fruit punch from Burger King?"

I'm pretty sure there's nothing special about the damn fruit punch but in this moment it was clearly a necessity of hers. About an hour later everyone came home. Lex was sleeping upstairs and I was watching T.V. so I could stay up to ensure that everyone made it back safe and sound. I was definitely *not* just watching Full House, I was ever so concerned as well. Before I went to bed, both my parents called to say goodnight in which Sesa and I both hit them with all that had occurred during this past day. My mom said she would make an appointment with our dentist for the upcoming Tuesday because that Monday was a holiday. And with that, we exchanged 'i love you's' and went to bed.

The next morning, as you can imagine, the celebration was continuing with breakfast at iHop. Everyone was showered and dressed while Lex was just barely getting up. Usually, she's one of the first ones downstairs and ready to go, but not today. After we practically pried her out of bed, she managed to snail her way to the bathroom to take a shower. A couple moments later we heard yells from the top of the stairs.

"Can you come upstairs and look at something" Lex called down to Sesa.

My curious George ass followed her upstairs as she was being summoned. At the top of the stairs was a towel dressed but still dripping wet from the shower Alexa, with a whole bunch or red dots on her underarms, shoulders, breasts and stomach. We stood and stared at the unknown that was covering her body. We assumed it some sort of allergic reaction to something, so she popped Benadryl and we sped off to the pancake house.

To say we had a breakfast fit for champions was to say the least. But hey, our boys *were* actual champions so, it technically made sense. Within the blink of an eye, everyone had empty plates expect for Alexa. She sat there with her blueberry compote pancakes in a stack, complied in front of her. Normally, once the compote on top of the pancakes ran out she was finished, but this time she didn't even touch it. At this point, everyone knew there was something very wrong. When asking Lex what the problem was and why she wasn't eating, she said that she felt nauseous and wasn't hungry. We decided to pack up her food for later and head back home.

We spent that Sunday evening watching movies; five out of the six of us did. Lex spent that Sunday evening sleeping…for 6 hours straight. We all assumed it was because the Benadryl made her drowsy but I figured that there was definitely more to that synopsis.

After movie day, I made lentils for dinner so we all could have one last meal together with the first time champions. That night, when I called for everyone to come to the table, I accompanied my yells from the living room to upstairs to wake Lex. She wobbled down the stairs, swaying from side to side. For someone who has never had alcohol, it sure as hell seemed as if she was drunk. She couldn't even walk straight. After finally reaching her 10 foot destination from the stairs to the dinner table, I told her I made Grammys lentils in which she refused to eat. Sesa and I told her that she had to eat *something* before she drove home because she hadn't eaten a thing all day. Within seconds of hearing that, she had nothing short of a temper tantrum at the table because "she wasn't hungry and all she wanted to do was go home."

"I am not going home with your Bambi ass, you can't even walk straight. I ain't driving with you" I said.

Her immediate response was crying of course. I told you it was common to cry for everything in this family and so she had to keep that tradition going. But this time, it was a different kind of cry. That night, the entire Lora family accompanied us on the drive home. Omar drove Alexa's car while she fell asleep, yet again, in the back of the car with Chris. Sesa drove her car with Nicky and I in company.

As soon as we got home, Lex sat on the couch and slowly knocked out. We again told my mom and dad about all of Alexa's excursions from today; from iHop, to the bed, to the dinner table, Oh My! They agreed to take her straight to our doctor the following morning, right after the dentist. However, that next morning was a school day and Alexa NEVER missed school. So, you could only imagine her reaction when dad told her that she was going to miss classes the following day so she could see our pediatrician. Well if you couldn't imagine, she cried, a lot.

6. DREADING MONDAY MORNING

On Tuesday morning, I woke up to Alexa sobbing into her pillow. I wasn't sure if she was crying because she was in pain or because she was missing school for the first time in forever. Maybe it was because she was going to her two favorite places, the dentist *and* the doctors office. Hopefully the sarcasm came across there. While I was in school, all I could think about was what was happening at those two appointments. I took out my phone in between classes in hope to see a text from my dad that was regarding an update on Lex, but instead, my phone stayed dry all day.

When school was over I ran across the street and hopped into my grandpa's car as quick as possible. I immediately asked him if he had talked to *anyone* at this point. Thankfully he spoke to my dad after both appointments were over and he had all the information ready for me.

He said that she had a bunch of tests done and one determined what would or would not happen at the dentist. This specific test showed the levels of her blood and platelet count and the results were that her platelets were extremely low. This ultimately wouldn't allow the dentist to do much for her if an incision needed to occur because of the low platelets. If they made an incision, there was a potential of her bleeding out because her blood wouldn't be able to clot like normal. So the decision was made to leave absolutely everything alone because any attempt at this wisdom tooth thing was just too much of a risk.

Wednesday came quickly, though as it arrived I honestly wished it would just slow down. I often don't remember much, but I vividly remember each and every aspect of this day. All went oddly well that morning, no hiccups involved. It was the last day before Thanksgiving break which meant that I got out of school at 12:30. Each class came as quickly as it left and soon enough the day was over. As it came to an end, the dismissal bell rang and my best friend Carly and I booked it to the main building and up the stairs to the second floor. We wanted to wish one of our favorite teacher Ms. Cordes, a Happy Thanksgiving before we left. As we were talking to her, the sole reason I attended TMLA jumped into our conversation. Mrs. Durkin, my art teacher, was always bringing laughs and joy to every room she walked into, but I don't think anything she or anyone said could of gotten me ready for what I was about to hear. I received a phone call from my mom and due to the entire day going so smoothly I completely forgot that the results from Alexa's test were supposed to come back today. Little did I know those results and that phone call would change all our lives forever.

I picked up the phone and all I could make out through my moms muddled speech and aggressive tears was that "Alexa's kidneys are dropping", followed by a loud dial tone. As confused as one could possibly be, I followed up such confusion by calling my dad in hopes that I could try to understand what was happening. When I called him and heard his voice, I knew there was something wrong. I asked him why mom was crying on the phone and questioned what exactly was happening to Alexa's kidneys.

"We got the results back and they told us that we have to rush to the emergency room because Alexa's kidneys are failing."

My mood has never shifted so rapidly. I was confused, scared, speechless, and so much more. I knew nothing about any of the information I was receiving. I didn't know about kidneys, what was involved in kidney failure, what happens when someone has kidney failure, etc. I felt clueless and helpless, probably the same as everyone else. At the same time, what I did know was that I couldn't stop thinking of Alexa and how she was feeling. I couldn't even begin to imagine what was going on in her mind right now. I knew her intelligence and knowledge on just about *everything* was forcing her mind to run a mile a minute, thinking about all the things that could possibly be wrong.

I ran over to Carly and told her we had to leave ASAP. We finished up our conversation as quickly as possible, gave them both a hug and kiss and practically jumped down the flights of stairs and rushed out the door. We made it to my grandpas car within seconds. I still didn't understand what was going on, not only with Lex but within myself. My head was spinning at this point but thankfully Carly was there to keep me as calm as possible. Once we got into the car, I immediately asked my grandpa if he had heard from anyone about anything and he confidently said "nope". Looks like we were both kind of in the dark this time, and in that moment it felt like the worst place in the world to be.

That afternoon, my grandpa and I drove to St. Francis Hospital in which I sprinted down the ever so familiar halls and up towards the ICU center. I asked for Alexa, and to my surprise, she was in the first room on my right. I walked in, as pensive as one could be because I didn't know what to expect. When the nurse slid open the sliding door and curtain, I vividly remember seeing my mom and dad sitting in chairs looking up at Lex while she sat in a hospital bed, calm as ever. Her eyes looked exhausted and her body portrayed stillness. I quickly got to questioning both of my parents; wanting to know all the information they received thus far. I needed to know it ALL.

My mom advised me that they were told to rush to the ER because Alexa's blood test results indicated that she was having kidney failure. Her counts stayed extremely low and that the "rash" that was covering her body was actually her blood vessels popping. All I could do while gathering this information was sit and listen. I was letting it all register in my brain as best as it possibly could. I didn't want to question them about what was going to happen because frankly, no one knew what was going to happen. So, I just followed what they were doing, sitting and waiting for the new test results that they took at the hospital.

We were all on the edge of our seats waiting for these results. It felt like the hours that passed were dragging on for days. All of our family was now in attendance; switching from the waiting room to the ICU room because only three people are allowed in at a time. As I was in the midst of swapping out with someone, I walked past a doctor that said Alexa's name and turned right back around to follow them into Alexa's room. Whoever was gonna switch out with me could wait a second. Finally, answers!

As he opened the door, everyone looked up from the floor and immediately stood up at his presence. He began telling us that they wanted to begin dialysis in attempt to regulate her kidney function. Also, they wanted to take a bone marrow sample later that evening so they could run a biopsy. We all nodded in approval and sat back down, remaining quiet. That night, Alexa had a local bone marrow scrape near her tailbone which was followed by countless hours of screaming due to the pain she was enduring. In addition to that came hourly finger pricks to check her sugar. In conclusion, that night was a complete disaster, bit it was unfortunately only the start of this rollercoaster ride.

That following day, everyone was back at the hospital waiting for the biopsy results. When the evening came, the results arrived as well. Nobody knew what to expect but we were hoping for positives, though what they gave us was nothing short of a nightmare. As the doctor walked in with the results, all I could remember was being scared out of my mind. No one knew what to think, how to feel, or how to act. While everyone thought about the future and what the "next step" was, I was daydreaming and reminiscing about what life was like just a couple of days prior when everything was "just fine". With that being said, reality started to set in when my distant hearing began to acknowledge the results and the long ass explanation of what was to come.

7. THE ROAD DOWNHILL

The bone marrow scrape results confirmed the diagnosis of Burketts Lymphoma. It was located primarily in the bone marrow, but without action it could spread rapidly. It's a very strong and aggressive form of cancer and due to its location in the body it could potentially become deadly. Appropriate action had to be taken as quickly as possible. As I looked around the room, everyone stood with emotionless expressions on their faces. My parents spoke with the doctors about where to go from here, what the next step was and what was going to be the easiest and most effective for Alexa and her current situation. He recommended going to Cohens Children's Hospital in which they would immediately begin her on dialysis in hope to save her kidneys. With that being said, the ambulance was called to transfer her and we all began packing up to be on our way.

As the paramedics prepared her for transport to Cohen's, they could clearly tell by the look on her face that Alexa was scarred as hell. So, to lighten the mood they played some music. They asked Lex who her favorite artist was and she immediately responded with Billy Joel. One of the EMT's whipped out his phone and had 'Piano Man' and 'We Didn't Start the Fire' blasting on the highest volume within seconds. We all started jamming out in the hospital hallways as we loaded all of our stuff into the cart to take downstairs. While my dads silly faces and constant jokes didn't seem to make Lex smile at this time of shock and confusion, the music made her crack a slight smile and that was all we all could've asked for.

My mom rode in the ambulance with Lex while my dad followed behind in his car. My grandpa and I were right on his tail as everyone else tagged along too. We all pulled up to Cohen's simultaneously. Lex was taken up to a room while we we all had to get registered in the system to receive a visitors pass. After checking in, taking the elevator ride up to her floor and walking around, turning every which way to find her room, we finally found her. The nurses were already prepping her to begin the dialysis. While expectations felt high because of the speedy transfer over, the first couple of nights of at Cohen's were a living nightmare. On Lex's third night of being hospital bound, I received a phone call from my Dad. The conversation that was coming when I accepted the phone call is one that I will remember for the rest of my life. Alexa called me from his phone crying hysterically, unable to speak through the sobbing. I couldn't exactly tell what was happening so my dad was quick to fill me in.

"The doctor came in tonight and told us that they want her body to rest. They're gonna induce her so that she is comatose."

Through the muffled tears Alexa yelled, "I love you and I'm sorry". I was firm in holding back my emotions as she continued to cry over the phone. I assured her that everything was going to be just fine because in all honesty, I knew about three words that my dad had said, all of them being the non-medical ones. "I love you too" were my final words back to her before the beep assured me that she hung up. A few hours later I got the call that she was sedated and laid in bed with a tube down her throat due to the lack of oxygen supply from her lungs. The sedation period was questionable; she had to wake herself up out if it. Therefore, this comatose period was going to make her become paralyzed from the neck down. Now if that's not a mouth full of traumatizing realness all at once, I don't know what is. Not only was it all occurring at once, but even worse it was happening to *my* sister. I swore that this couldn't be happening to me, to her, to our family. I never realized that in the blink of an eye, your world could quite literally come crumbling down on you.

She ended up being in a coma for about three months. Those three months consisted of no movement, no talking, no vision, no eating… nothing. The doctors continued to reiterate to us that if and when she wakes up, it would have to be on her own. They couldn't do anything to force her to wake up because it could be harmful, especially because they weren't quite sure about everything that was wrong with her yet. Those three months were just a waiting game. It was probably the scariest period throughout her entire journey. "If she wakes up" replayed in my head from the moment I woke up to the second my head touched the pillow. Each night when I came to visit, I prayed that there would be some sort of change, that I would see her eyes begin to open or that she would say

"Hey Dee" as I strolled in with homemade dinner for my mom and dad. However, I was greeted with nothing but silence each and every day. I watched her lay with her eyes closed, her soft hands filling with water because of the dialysis, and her mouth being forced open by tubes. That's a state that no one wants to see their loved one in.

Although she was in this terrible physical condition, I was weirdly always comforted when I walked into her room. Walking into her room was like walking into a museum filled with our family and friends' love. Cute little picture frames, teddy bears, and gift baskets filled with just about anything you could imagine, lined the windowsills and spilled on the chairs and floors. Everything was awaiting for Lex to wake up and admire. While those material things brought me comfort, knowing that we all weren't in this alone felt even greater. However as her room continued to overflow with love, I couldn't get one dark cloud out of my mind. The hospital monitors that she was constantly hooked up too. The loud beeps and constant rings always sent my heart into a parallel universe. Any sudden noise made me think that something was going to explode. I was clearly knee deep in hospital shows and movies that my mind was getting away from itself. However, after a few weeks of sending my heart into my stomach, I was finally getting used to not only the beeps and rings, but the atmosphere as well. Unfortunately, seeing my sister in that way did not manage to lighten me up but I tried to constantly stay as positive as possible.

During the months that Alexa was induced, a lot went on "behind the scenes". Within the first few weeks of word getting out to "the public", our entire family received tons of messages and calls from family, friends, neighbors, and so many more. Everyone was reaching out to us and sending their love, prayers, and support. It was definitely overwhelming, but a good kind of overwhelming. When it's generated through so much love, it's all one could ask for and so much more. I for one, first hand experienced the support due to always being around and having my family be so well known at just about everywhere. From school, to my grandpas house in Whitestone, to the supermarket, and all the way around the social media world and back. At this point *everyone* knew. Word gets around pretty quick, especially through social media. It it truly such an incredible thing that I will forever be grateful for because hundreds of messages poured in each and every day for Lex and our entire family. Every person that showed an ounce of concern for us during this difficult time was a genuine blessing. It showed me how far love could stretch, from people we see everyday to a familiar face on the block. Both the good and the bad seemed so surreal.

While continuing to receive this immense amount of love, reality was that Lex wasn't doing much better. The amount of IV's in her arms increased as well as the bags of medicine and fluid that was constantly being hung up and run through her body. Throughout the entirety of the time she was induced, she had very little improvement. However, when there was any positive spark in sight, we took it and ran. For a couple of weeks, things began to stabilize. Until one night when nurses stormed into her room after hearing each and every one of her monitors scream. Alexa's heart rate dropped to zero. They were quick to begin chest compressions in hope to revive a practically lifeless body. Though just as they were about to forcefully begin the pumping, her heart monitor stopped screeching and her pressure began rising. If you didn't think she was weird before, how about now! If you can only imagine my parents' hearts being in their stomachs for the remainder of the night, just a wink of sleeping was in their near future.

The following day consisted of nurses coming in and out of her room five times more than usual. No one was quite sure why that scary episode occurred the night prior but to ensure that it would never occur again they decided to move her to the PICU floor for the next couple of weeks. Thankfully there was never another massive fluctuation in her heart rate during those 2 weeks of being there. The doctors and nurses then decided to ease up on the visits and monitor her as they normally would on the hospital floor.

Near the end of January we started to see some light. Alexa's eyes began to open more and more each day. Although she was still slightly sedated, she was undoubtedly forcing her eyes to open. At first instance she was frightened at the sight of a massive tube protruding out of her mouth. Everything that has happened since she was put out was all new to her: the tubes, the machines, her current state, everything. While *we* all had some time to adapt to this new but temporary condition, she had yet to even experience it. After she quickly noticed the tube, she then began to notice the lack of feeling that she had from her neck down. I could see the confusion in her face whenever she woke up from a couple of hours of resting. She would search for the bedsheets and try to grasp them in hope to feel something. Though with a brain as big as Alexa's, she slowly began to piece together her condition within just hours after opening her eyes for the first time. Soon after the puzzle pieces were finally in place, her doctors and nurses' check ins would allow her to gather more information, which allowed her to prove her assumptions correct. Each time they would come in to check up on her, change a medicine bag or simply check her vitals, she would glance at the label to see what kind of meds she was on, look at her pressure to ensure it was good and so on and so forth. Even in that state she managed to become some form of independent which genuinely blows my mind. The thing that hit her the most after waking up was being told how much time had passed while she was sedated. It was difficult for her to comprehend that within all that time, she was practically lifeless. It wasn't much better when she was then realizing that so much had changed so quickly. A 19 year old young woman who was beginning her life in college, pursuing her dreams with friends and family alongside, and managing her way through this crazy world, to then waking up and looking at a room full of machines, tubes, and needles coming at you from every which way. Needless to say, that was a tough pill to swallow.

Within time, her oxygen intake increased which then allowed them to remove the tube. Though it was not high enough to have her breath on her own just yet. Her doctors decided it was best to insert a trachea into her throat which allowed for another air breathing passage towards the lungs. The trachea would also permit her to slowly regain movement as well as continue therapy in a more "normal" way. The people that pushed her to work harder each and everyday in therapy was her incredible nurses.Often times at night, reality would set in to Lex's head. When there was not much going on around her, her brain would begin focusing on her new reality. With a frown on a usually always smiling face, her nurses were always quick to realize what was encompassing her mind so they would casually pop in and joke around while checking her vitals. You simply couldn't ever be upset when you were around the nurses at Cohen's because they were all so spectacular. From the doctors, nurses, security guards, and even the front desk folks that tend to all your possible questions, it was very apparent that we gained a new family there.

As the three month sedation continued to wear off day by day, Lex's doctors began to discuss chemotherapy treatments that would benefit her and her diagnosis. However they didn't have much time to evaluate a chemo schedule because of the time crunch she was on. Having lost so much time with the dialysis and sedation, they needed to format a quick but effective plan. With that in mind, they decided to start a treatment that would be effective but only to a certain extent. It consisted of a couple of weeks of treatment followed by a few days of her body recuperating. After situating the plan, they decided that it was best to receive this chemo in a different facility, one that granted her the ability to receive the chemotherapy and continue her progress with physical and occupational therapy. However, this seemingly magical place that could provide her with the best of both worlds was in New Jersey.

In all honesty, it didn't take us long to come to a conclusion that the hospital in NJ would be what was best for Alexa and her health. That weekend, my parents and I visited Robert Wood Johnson University Hospital and Children's Specialized Hospital in New Brunswick, New Jersey. We wanted to see first hand where Lex was going and what kind of seemingly incredible treatment she would be receiving. After a complete tour of both sides of the hospital we were sure that it would be a perfect fit for her. Now the only aspiration was that she would hopefully would have a perfectly smooth journey here.

With that being taken care of, we then drove back to NY to shower her with information and pictures of what would be her home for the next couple of months. I sat on her bed and told her about all the cool things they had to offer her. Her favorite was the pool that she would eventually be able to go into after she was a little more advanced in her therapy sessions. She was excited to start her journey there while I was beyond scared to continue it. I knew the nerves were all the more reason to trust in her and look forward towards her future.

Before Alexa was transferred to NJ they had stopped the chemotherapy treatment that she was receiving at Cohens. She was said to be in remission at the time, though she never finished her cycle. Lex only had about a week left at Cohens before she left and within that week our family had yet again one last but huge decision to make. Receiving chemo through spinal taps long term at RWJ would be difficult because of Alexa's mass.

Therefore, it could potentially cause long term damage. The "fix" was to insert an ommaya in her head so that receiving chemo was easier and less destructive. The ommaya would be barely visible as it would be implanted under her scalp. It was solely there to benefit her in receiving treatments with no harm. While this was a difficult decision to make because of the later risk that it had, the greater risk was the spinal taps that could effect her current rehabilitation and movement forever. Alexa was considered underage because she was only 19, so my parents had the final decision. Coming to a conclusion for something as big as this was one of the hardest decisions this far, especially for them. Not only did they already feel as helpless as the rest of us because there was nothing in their power that they could do to protect Lex, but they also had to make life altering decisions like this, with the potential of the outcome being positive and/or negative. The decision that was made, led us to helplessly waiting for Alexa to come out of surgery, the most uneasy feeling in the entire world.

8. NJ, HERE WE COME

We sat and waited. I was a nervous wreck all day because while the rest of my family was able to get to their phones and make a call for updates, I was in school taking a freaking English test. That was just about the last thing that I wanted to focus on, but I tried my best to concentrate. I knew if I failed a test, Alexa would literally find a way to get up and smack me right across the face. My mind was racing a mile a minute for the entire day, thinking about anything and everything that could go every which way. Later that evening I was finally able to visit Lex. On the elevator ride up, I couldn't stop thinking about how she was going to feel: physically, emotionally and mentally. It was easy to understand how my family and I felt because we were all in the same position. We were bystanders who couldn't do much of anything to free her from this horrible situation. She was the one that was dealing with all of this nonsense in every which way possible. If what she had already been through wasn't enough, now she had a god damn thing being stuck up inside her head. What the hell was next, reconstructing her organs?! My hypochondriac self couldn't express to you how many emotions I was feeling underneath my semi smiling face.

As I made my way down the hall, I passed by a bunch of our nurse friends. Each time I passed by a nurse that I knew or that knew me, we would always stop to catch up for a brief moment or smile and wave as we passed each other. Their joy was always infectious, even after long days of constant work. I could barely handle walking through the pediatric unit to get to Alexa's room. I was always holding back tears cause I was walking through a zone where children, often times babies and those younger than me, were fighting these battles that were unfairly given to them. Seeing the nurses smile as I walked past them comforted me because although I knew the situation the children were in was anything but easy, I knew that they were in the greatest hands possible. Knowing that if I or someone in my family couldn't be there 24/7, Alexa would always have someone there for her.

My initial intention was to try not to stare. I wasn't sure what I would be staring at anyway because I didn't even know where I was looking. As I walked into her room, I noticed her eyes were sealed shut. She was still out from the anesthesia. I was hoping to walk into her room and see smiles and hear laughter, assuring me that everything went well during the surgery and she was fine but instead, there was silence. I couldn't help but notice her sleeping face and swollen body while it lay on the hospital bed. It gave me a sense of PTSD because I couldn't help but flashback to the few months prior when she was in an ever so similar state. I walked past Lex's bed and brought my parents the dinner I made for them, chicken cutlets and rice with a side of hugs and kisses. As they ate, I stared. I walked over to her bed and watched over her as innocently as possible. I knew that if I radiated any negative thoughts or energy from my brain to hers that she would somehow sense it, wake up, and kick my ass. It was the telepathy thing, ya know? So I stood, attempted to attain all my thoughts, fears and worries to myself and held her hand while I began to pray.

As I prayed, millions of things flooded my head though none of them were about her condition and what she was going through. I was thinking about all of the time that I was spending *away* from her. For sisters that are 3-4 years apart, some would think that we wouldn't be as close as we are. However we have practically been one in the same for as long as I can remember. I absolutely hated not being able to spend my days at the hospital with her as well as comforting my mom who never left her side. I hated only being able to see them both for about an hour or less each night. I hated this whole situation honestly, which I'm sure just about anyone could understand and agree with. It really sucked. Personally it seemed like life in itself was falling apart for me and I didn't exactly know how to clean it up and make it better, but I sure as hell knew I had to try.

Before I left that night, I squeezed Lex's hand for a while in hope that she would respond or show some sign of waking up, but unfortunately I got nothing. The following day when she was bright eyed and busy tailed, her nurses kept a close eye on her. The next few days were crucial in terms of watching how her body responded to the placement of the ommaya. They had to monitor her actions to ensure that the positioning didn't affect any part her brain. Thankfully all was well and those days went as smooth as could be. Transfer day was on that upcoming weekend and everyone was preparing. Bags were being packed, things were being brought home and/or moved to NJ and final checkups were being done until the very moment she was rolled into the ambulance.

Leaving Cohens was super emotional for Lex and my mom. Not only were they leaving the place that had helped Lex so much in such a short but seemingly long journey thus far, but they were also leaving their new family. The love, warm wishes and prayers we received throughout the entirety of that 'first round' hospital journey was incredible, something we all will never forget.

9. HOSPITAL...ROUND 2

When the ambulance pulled up to Robert Wood Johnson, Lex was instantly situated in her own room while nurses encircled and evaluated her. The evaluation involved multiple blood tests and several IV placements. One line was connected to the port that was on her chest and two lines were being placed on her arm. During all that miserable work, my mom was busy situating herself in their 'new place' for the extent of their stay there. Once they were both settled in at the best of their abilities, Alexa's main nurse for the night walked in with a lengthy list consisting of an adjusted chemotherapy treatment plan. Though she was 'in remission' they wanted to begin chemo immediately to ensure that everything would stay suppressed. Therefore, the following day would be Lex's first day of receiving this new treatment as well as her first time receiving through the ommaya. The plan she was put on was a two weeks on and two weeks off cycle. She would be receiving chemo for 14 days and recovering on the opposite side of the hospital, Children's Specialized, receiving rehab for the following 14 days. However, there was a slight catch to this whole process. Each chemo treatment would progressively get stronger than the last. This would cause her to potentially have an increase in side effects. With that being said, she was only able to transfer to the rehab side if she was well enough. Although it is not widely known to have subtle effects when someone with cancer is undergoing chemotherapy, our fingers and toes were crossed that these treatments were as painless and easygoing as possible. The hope was to move on with this chapter of her life so she can open up a new one, a blank page.

The first two weeks of treatment began and all went smoothly. My mom and Alexa spent the following two weeks adjusting to their second 'home away from home' on the rehab side. After a semi-quick transition, they were finally somewhat settled. Alexa's first task in rehab was relearning

40

how to swallow. A trachea is positioned in such a way that your voice box has to be moved in order to allow a passage for air. Therefore, you must relearn how to do the basics, swallow, talk, chew, etc. During this time, she was also beginning to move her fingers and toes independently. As her fist two weeks came to a conclusion, Lex was just about able to talk, swallow her saliva, and move not only her fingers and toes, but her hands and legs as well. Those first few days were an eye opener as to what Lex was capable of doing, as long as she kept that vivid and hopeful mindset. When everyone heard about the immense progress she made in such a short time, we were all amazed and beyond proud. We knew that between the motivation she had to get up and walk out of the hospital, along with the massive amount of support she had backing her up, she would be running out of there and back to NY in no time. Now, it was back to the hospital to continue chemo, through this time it was not so pleasant. These two weeks were filled nausea, stomachaches and joint pain. The constant rejection of chemo resulted in her constantly throwing up just about anything she consumed, which wasn't very much at all. Even smells made her nauseous. These were all new experiences and feelings Alexa had, but thank goodness for our solid as a rock momma who effortlessly rolled with all the punches. She held her hand and stuck by her side from the very first day, a couple of bumps wasn't going to change that. Lex was always comforted because when she woke up and looked over at my mom, she was there with a smile streaming across her face.

While there was so much progress in the first few weeks of Lex being in NJ, there was also a major upset to having both her and mom being so far away. My dad and I were unfortunately only able to *physically* them on the weekends. On Friday's after he left work, he would drive to my grandmas house to pick me up so we could begin our journey to New Brunswick together to visit them. I was able to spend a couple of hours there on Friday night before Sesa would pick me up to spend the weekend at her house in Rutherford. It was only about a half an hour away which allowed us to go back and visit on Saturday for dinner. Then, she would return me and my expensive ass on Sunday mornings.

On the other hand, my dad was able to stay at the hospital throughout the entire weekend which was always great. He was able to accompany them both but he didn't receive such privilege with ease. The sleeping 'arrangements' were nothing short of the most uncomfortable situation ever. They shared a twin size bed amongst themselves each night. To say that they slept a total of 4 hours each night was a complete overstatement. However, I can firmly say that they would sleep standing up if they had too, anything for Alexa. While the whole visiting situation was slightly frustrating because I couldn't spend the time I wanted to with my family, I soaked up the time I did get. I also took advantage of Alexa not being ever so busy with her own school work so she could help take care of mine.

Basically above all the other things I needed Alexa's help with, I really needed help with all my 'college stuffs'. Senior year brought massive amounts of "college talk" and information, from on-sight interviews to college apps and portfolios needing to be done. I needed *my person* to keep my head straight. I found solace in those few hours being us time, filing through my college apps and filling up my heart. As much as I needed my second brain, I knew this was a somewhat of a safe haven for her as well. Once we ended our education filled adventure for the weekend, the rest of Lex's week consisted of chemo continuing to kill this horrible thing called cancer.

Time passed by pretty quickly while Lex was in NJ because of the small amount of time we spent together. After about a month of constant training with the trachea, Lex was able to fully speak and swallow pureed foods. Everyone's jaw continued to drop in shock of how quickly she progressed, though Lex wasn't phased. She knew that every day there was constant progress meant being one step closer to heading home.

At this point in her stay at RWJ and CHS, both my mom and Alexa had made countless more 'nurse friends' just like she did at Cohnes. She was always down to give some of her nurses, specifically on the rehab side, a tough time because let's be honest, what kind of fun is it to be the 'easy going' patient. Kraig, one of her all time favorite nurses, came to give her meds at night on the days that she was his patient. She constantly refused them, not because she didn't want to take them, just because she wanted to give him a tough time. Of course, he would always feed into her stupidity and roll his eyes a bunch before he put on a one-man show just to get her to take the medicine. Being there and watching her laugh and get a little bit of her sass back always made me smile. It was a sign that although some things may have changed, she was getting better. It was a step in the right direction and that was all that mattered. Kraig would always be down to crack a joke and make Alexa smile, even on the days where she wasn't up to being silly. He always knew what to do to lift her spirits. He even had his own WWE inspired entrance for when he walked into her room. If he didn't abide by the 'entrance rules' he had to go back outside and re-enter. It was all fun and games because nurses like him are what keep patients like Alexa going, especially childhood cancer patients. He was a genuine light during Lex's entire journey in NJ. On days where Alexa wasn't his patient, he would manage to pop in for a quick hello. That drop by would always be accompanied by Lex saying, "and you're not my nurse today becauseeeee…", which was then followed by a subtle eye roll. His smile, his laugh, his attitude, his entire will to be a nurse and care for not only the patient, but their families as well, is something that no one could ever forget.

The incredible people didn't stop there. Alexa's go to girls and chit chat buddies were nurse Taylore Fritzinger, Willisa Turner-Warren and Nicole Forsythe. Taylore did all the fun activities with Lex. My dad called her Tinker Bell because she was always peppy and practically flying around the floor like there was pixie dust trailing at her feet. It also didn't help that you could just about literally fit her in your pocket. She always had the brightest smile on her face and that was what made everyone feel so comfortable and loved around her. Taylore and Lex made a dream box for 2018, since she arrived there jut a few weeks after the new year. They filled the box with paper slips that read all of 'Alexa's dream and wishes' for the new year. It allowed her to keep focused on what her goals were; those dreams needed to turn into realties. She also always kept Lex's room decorated with inspirational quotes and messages from her and other nurses to encourage her to strive towards the finish line. She taped them to just about every flat surface that was in her room. Nurses Willisa and Nicole also pushed Alexa to reach for the stars. They encouraged her the most when she was beginning her journey to walk again. I vividly remember them clapping and having their own little party each time Lex walked around the hospital floor. Once she managed to walk without having to take a break, she took everyone on a stroll. She took them to one of her favorite places, the recreation center. Chris and Nicky were her first walking buddies. They may have fallen in love with that place because of the amount of games and toys it had to offer. Each time they came to visit, the three of them beelined to the rec-room to go play.

While Lex began to get comfortable with being in a new hospital with different people, she also started to find some interest in the activities they were offering. Alexa was the last person to want to go to an 'event'. However, she had overheard that they were hosting a prom night for all the patients in the hospital. Everyone would be able to dress up, eat some non-hospital food, spend time together with their loved ones, and make some new friends. Ultimately everyone would be able to have a night off, filled with no dawning on the situation that they're in or what they are going to have to endure tomorrow. It was a night to decompress for all the children that were struggling in the fight of their lives.

When I visited Lex that weekend she was telling me all about it. She asked if I could bring her the prom dress she wore for her prom a couple months back. As she continued talking, I noticed the excitement in her face, something I hadn't seen in a long time. With all the stress before hand from school and now this, she needed a night to relax and 'let loose'. She was determined to be there, all done up with her prom dress on and her makeup done. Yeah, she even asked me to do her makeup! Of course that made my year because not only did she never wear makeup but she asked me to do it for her. It was like TMLA prom 2016 all over again and I was so excited. I called my mom on that Thursday to check up on Lex and see how they both were holding up. She unfortunately provided me with news that they weren't having the best week.

"I don't think Lex is going to be able to go" she said.

My heart instantly broke. I knew how excited she was and I couldn't even begin to imagine how much it sucked for her to hear that she possibly couldn't attend. She wasn't able to enjoy herself because of this stupid disease that was constantly making her feel like shit and now one night wouldn't even slide! Her nurses were scared of her contracting an infection because of how low her counts were. The mass of people that were attending was not helping the situation either. With that being said, Lex went on a mission. She tried her absolute best to eat foods that would make her counts go up in hope that she could attend the celebration. It was Friday night and the final verdict was in. Her counts just weren't high enough. The disappointment in her eyes was the worst on that Saturday night. To somewhat make up for the upset in her eyes, I asked Sesa if we could bring Buffalo Wild Wings to the hospital and have a mini party in her room. We bought wings her way and spent a couple hours relaxing and playing tons of card games after dinner. It was the best in-room hospital prom EVER and I hope Lex felt the same way.

As the days and weeks seemed to pass almost effortlessly, March rolled around in an instant. My mom and Alexa continued their everyday battles and constant hard work. I, on the other hand, was busy working on Lex's big 20th birthday surprise. Being in the hospital is hard. Being in the hospital with cancer is even worse. Being in the hospital with cancer on your birthday has to take the cake. I knew not all of our family and friends could be there to celebrate Lex's 20th, but I wanted to make it a special one for her. Going through this battle and fighting to see tomorrow often puts a dark aura around a person. I wanted to lighten the mood and bring my sister a little piece of home that she hasn't seen or been able to *really* experience in months. With that in mind, I contacted all of our family and friends. By all, I mean basically everyone that has ever made an impact in our lives. That list strung from family, Alexa's friends, my friends, our middle school teachers and principal, our TMLA family and so much more. Everyone that has been involved and apart of our blessed lives thus far were elated to participate and in celebrating Alexa. I asked them to send me a video of them saying happy birthday in addition to a small message or a memory that they both shared. The hope was that she would be able to remember the times when everything wasn't so awful. The goal was to make her cry happy tears, though with my family it wasn't going to be difficult. I just wanted her to smile a bit more because as each day continued to get harder, I felt like she needed a little spark of encouragement to keep going.

A couple of sleepless nights editing the shit out of the video, it was finally ready for her birthday on March 16th. That Friday before my dad and I headed out to NJ, we passed by La Cheesecake to pick up Lex's favorite; a marble cheesecake, half blueberry and half plain. We had them write: "Happy 20th Birthday Lex" in blue icing, right smack in the middle. I clutched my iPad to my chest the entire car ride because I was so damm excited to see Alexa and my families reaction to my surprise. An hour and a half trip later and we were finally at RWJ. I left my dad in smoke as I ran to the front door, up the elevator and into her room. I walked into a party that was going on without me. I was surprised to see that some of Alexa's friends came to surprise her too. A room filled with love burst out by the seams and she was so happy!

After we sang happy birthday and cut the cake, Lex began to open her presents. Last but not least was me! I pulled out my iPad and gave her a little bit of a background story on what the heck she was about to watch before I pressed play. Everyone in the room was staring at that screen for the entire 30 minutes doing nothing but sobbing. Alexa gave me the biggest hug ever and thanked me a million times that day. It was definitely a birthday for the books to me, and I hope it was one that Alexa will never forget.

As her birthday wrapped up for the night, it was back to reality for the next couple of days before hopefully being able to transfer back to CSH for some more rehab. Thankfully that following week she was able to transfer over. However, she was not as lucky for the few weeks following. She stayed in RWJ having just about the worst time one could imagine. Those weeks felt endless for both my mom and Alexa. Even though I was only there on the weekends, I felt like they stayed on the hospital side for months. As each week progressed with the same result, not being well enough to transfer, Lex began to feel tired of fighting. The chemo was definitely getting to her at this point. Though, Alexa's 'mama nurse' Sue, made sure that she would never stop fighting no matter where this life took her. She whipped her ass into shape real quick. Sue was the painless blood sugar lady who helped Lex get every ounce of PT in that she possibly could. Even a few minutes of moving while she was getting medicine for the night or getting her sheets changed was enough for her to be content with. Everything counted in Sue's eyes and it genuinely was a hundred percent true. Her smile and laugh was as contagious as her swift attitude. She helped both Alexa, my mom and our entire family in more ways than one. She was always there whenever anyone needed anything, wether she was Alexa's nurse that day or not. She constantly gave our family hope. Although there were days that felt like we were taking 10 steps back, there were also going to be days where we will be taking 20 steps forward. Those are the ones that we had to be thankful for and look forward too.

10. WE'RE ALMOST THERE...

As time carried on, Lex continued to have some good days and some shitty days. Though no matter what the day had to offer, she was always smiling. You would never catch her with a frown on her face. Even on the days where it felt like nothing went right and there seemed to be no way to escape this dark tunnel, she smiled through it. No matter how difficult and how trying times were, Lex always kept her head up in each and every situation that she was, for some reason, thrown into. That smile brought a sunny side to April. She was not only continuing her walking journey but she was introducing herself to longer distances with less breaks. She was also feeling well enough to be able to transfer back and forth almost every two weeks. When she was told she couldn't attend rehab because of her low counts, she didn't let that stop her from keeping up with her PT and OT. On the weekdays she would have limited therapy and on the weekend she had none at all. She wasn't depending on her therapists' to help her do everything, she knew she had to do something too. Lex began to push herself even harder because she was feeling better and knew she had to take the good days and run...literally. It was as if the switch was flipped and all the lights were shinning bright in that once terribly dark tunnel. Seeing the other side was clear as day. Though another drop in this rollercoaster ride was rudely approaching us.

When my dad and I drove to NJ on Fridays, we brought some homemade food with us. We got to the hospital and saw both Lex and my mom playing Skip-Bo, of course. We all sat and talked while they chomped down on their dinner. Sesa was picking me up later and she was being joined by Thing 1 and Thing 2, Chris and Nicky. A few hours following dinner, they strolled in. The boys hugged Lex and gave her the look, the "are you thinking what I'm thinking" look. Within seconds, Skip-Bo cards were being passed around the room again. As Chris dealt the cards Lex finished her dinner in bed and continued her conversation with Sesa. She was bringing her up to speed on all the progress she had made in the past week. However at one point during their chat, Lex seemed to tune out. It was as if she was looking into space but couldn't regain focus. Sesa began calling out her name to get her attention but she didn't respond. She poked at her arm and started nudging her leg.

"Alexa! Lexi! Are you okay. What's wrong?"

Within seconds she began to shake. Everyone got up in a panic and rushed to her bedside. Sesa ran out the door and yelled.

"Someone come help! Help! I think she's having a seizure!"

A nurse rushed in and acknowledged her seizing state and immediately called for backup and a doctor. They rushed everyone out of the room except for my mom. I, being a great listener, took it upon myself to stay in the room as well. Only a few seconds passed before more nurses and a doctor blasted through the doorway. Those seconds felt like hours, but they quickly proceeded with protocol. The nurses kept her arms and legs pinned down as much as possible while the doctor quickly prepared the syringe loaded with hope. As she continued to shake uncontrollably, I couldn't bear to look down at her helpless face. Her eyes screamed "make it stop". I tried my best to hold onto her legs and not look at her but she kept turning her head and looking directly at me. My goodness I wish I could have stopped all that trauma in an instant. I can't help but constantly recall and replay that exact moment in my head. When it first occurred, each time I closed my eyes, that moment played over and over again in my head. Sometimes I wish I would have listened and left the room when I was told too because recalling that sight is truly traumatizing. At the same time I feel like I needed to be there. She needed hope and I tried to give her some. As we continued to watch her body seize, the doctor finally inserted the syringe into her arm. She instantly began to calm down. Her body stopped shaking, her eyes were no longer rolled back, and her breathing slowed down.

"Everything will be okay. Just keep breathing and relax" my mom continued to whisper in her ear.

We all watched her slowly come back to us. Not much time passed before the next seizure came along. A second fucking seizure and nobody knew why the hell it was happening. I couldn't watch another one so I stepped out. The nurse closed the door behind me and I ran to the nearest seat. I threw myself onto the couch and began to cry uncontrollably. I couldn't manage to keep it in this time. I felt all eyes on me when everyone looked up from having their head in their hands to stare at me. As my sobs got louder, I could feel myself being surrounded so I knew not to look up. This wasn't the *me* that everyone knew.

So many things were going through my head at that moment. I couldn't escape what I just witnessed. I was so thankful that the boys didn't see what I just saw. Both my dad and Sesa nudged me to ensure that I was okay. They consoled me by rubbing my back and head while they cried with me. My attention needing self would normally love that, but this time I didn't want it. Thankfully Chris and Nicky knew exactly what I needed and that was hugs. Lucky for me, they give the best ones.

The few minutes of waiting after the second seizure fell like an eternity. Five minutes later, the door slowly opened and everyone started to file out. We were all *literally* on the edge of our seats. As the doctor walked out, we all stood up at once. He exchanged his idea of what could have possibly occurred, with us. Though he was not going to be sure unless they took tests so he could view from the inside what transpired. He was having her be transferred to the ICU so she could be monitored for the next couple of days. Him and my dad shook hands while Sesa and I peeked into the room where they were already getting ready to move her. As the nurses rolled her stretcher out of the room and off the floor, we all stayed behind to pack up.

We loaded everything up on a cart and rolled it into the room they were giving her in the ICU. As we made it to her new stay, we were informed that she was already getting her first scan. They were taking an electrophalagram of her brain which would determine if there was any trauma brought about from the seizures. It would also show what had caused them to occur.

Silence seemed to the the theme of the night. Mostly because none of us were sure what we had just witnessed. We went from talking and having a family dinner to being in the ICU with possible brain damage within two hours.

After about an hour of waiting ever so patiently, Lex arrived at the door. She laid in her hospital bed with her eyes closed and her hands at her sides. The EEG process consisted of her having a sock like cap put on her head to track her brain movement. Its purpose was to continue monitoring her brain activity throughout the next few days. She was going to be hooked up to another machine that involved a camera recording her movements. If a seizure was approaching, it could be read before it occurred with the help of the sensors underneath the cap.

Before I left that night, Lex started to wake up with a bit more focus than she had prior, but that didn't last long. Since her dinner was cut short, she needed to eat. However, she was still a bit shaky so my mom decided to spoon feed her the remainder of her dinner. Lex opened her mouth to receive the food, my mom fed her, she closed her mouth, and stayed still.The problem there was her not chewing her food. She simply closed her mouth and continued to keep it closed for minutes on end. That was definitely something new and so we were awfully confused.

"Chew and swallow so you could eat more" my mom kept saying.

Lex shook her head in approval and looked back up towards the TV. With the brain trauma that she just endured, it was easy to understand that she may not be "all here" at the moment. It was a confusing concept at first but understandable. The part of her brain that controlled things such as chewing or swallowing, seemed to of been disrupted which is why she wasn't following "directions" per say. After about 10 minutes of consistently encouraging her to swallow the food, she finally did. The amount of patience we all didn't acquire that night did not help one bit. It felt like things were just happening at this point and no one had a definite answer for anything. It was all up in the air. Everything felt like it was going to hell and if our family felt it, I'm positive Lex sure as hell did.

The next few days in the ICU were critical. Since returning from having the brain scan, she was put on a medicine that would slow down or prevent any possible seizures. Two days later the results would come in and although we were all curious and excited, feeling excited over such a thing felt like a crime.

The results showed that there was a spill of the chemo medicine, methotrexate. It seemed to of overflowed out of the ommaya in which it was inserted in. The buildup caused an overdosage of methotrexate which then caused her body to react negatively in terms of killing the cancer cells. This treatments purpose was more to suppress her "nonexistent cells" because she was still said to be in remission. However, this spillage caused

51

more harm than anticipated. Not only did it cause seizures but it may have also caused her cancer to return because there was no suppressing being done. She also continued to have no immune system to fight off the idea of even one cancer cell returning. Her lack of immune system would only allow cells to multiple. Due to her ommaya failing and causing such a hassle, they obviously no longer treated her through that access. Alexa then had to resort to the more dangerous method, the spinal taps. The only reason it wasn't *as* frowned upon as it was prior was because of her weight lose. Being in the hospital with months of not being able to eat properly, though still receiving nutrients, caused Lex to loose a ton of weight. With that being said, her doctors were quick to formulate a new plan. First they needed to take and evaluate more tests and scans to determine if she had relapsed. If she did, did it spread? They needed answers just about as quick as we wanted them. Not being able to physically be there was annoying enough but receiving all this information over the phone seemed to be worse. Although I'm sure my mom felt it the most, trying to be there for Alexa and remain as strong as possible while Lex constantly questioned life.

"Why did God chose this battle for me" was all that she said whenever she was feeling at her lowest.

As positive as she always tried to stay, she had her off days as well. If you thought things couldn't possibly get worse, buckle up because a whole bunch of crazy that's about to aboard this ride.

Alexa's doctors and nurses continued to follow her brain activity with the help of the sock puppet that was attached to her head. Whenever my dad or I cracked that joke, she smiled a bit. I couldn't help seeing her this way. I felt like I wasn't even looking at my sister. I wish that was something no one ever has to say, let alone think. But here I am writing it. Although she didn't look quite the same, I knew somewhere deep down was my High School Musical singing karaoke buddy. I just knew she had it in her. As I hoped and prayed every day that this nightmare would end, it seemed to of only begun. Her numerous full body CT scams showed her being positive for new cancer cells. She had relapsed. This time, it was leukemia in her bone marrow.

I'm not sure I would have taken this news as well as I did if I was there in person. I somewhat swallowed it and hoped that I would wake up from this nightmare. As my mom continued to cry on the phone, I looked at

Alexa while on FaceTime and watched her shake her head in agreence. It was as if she was accepting the fact that it had returned and she was just going to have to work harder to kill this shit, this time for good. I did nothing but smile while my insides dropped to the floor. How could she be so okay with doing this again?! I couldn't seem to wrap my head around it the first time but here we are *again* and she was 100% ready for it.

Insane is the only word that came to my head. This was nothing that was going to be solved overnight. My God, I hope to grow a motivation like that because it's truly the attitude I think *everyone* needs. Although her first time felt like it lasted forever and took her to hell and back, she was ready for round two, no need for breaks in between. It was as if anything this child faced would be going down because of her determination and we were all here to witness her superiority.

The next few days Lex was finally able to be relieved from the sock puppet festivities and move into a "less watched" section of the ICU. Though she was still checked on every so often, it was less frequent. It was her last stop until she was able to go back to her usual room on the regular side of the hospital.

It was finally Friday which meant that my dad and I were off to NJ. We got there early because we both had off from work and school. We had arrived at around 4pm which allowed us to have the whole evening to ourselves, just the four of us together, like it used to be! The first couple of minutes, we were fully updated with what happened during the past couple of days.

Lex was begging to lean off the dosage of seizure meds that she was receiving. She was also able to chew and swallow again without being in such pain and confusion. Overall it was a pretty good few days. Both my mom and dad left the room a short time after to get us all lunch. In the meantime, Lex and I had some long awaited and much needed sister time!

She told me that she was currently enlisted to become a *Make A Wish* child in hope that one of her dreams would potentially come true with the help of this incredible organization. *Make A Wish* is a nonprofit that helps fulfill the wishes of children with critical illnesses. So ideally we discussed all the possible outcomes of this so called "wish". Would it be: seeing and meeting her favorite country artist Luke Bryan, meeting the entire Marvel cast, going on a trip to Italy…the wishes were endless. It was a conversation

I will ever forget because in that moment I genuinely felt like I had my sister back. It was a rough patch trying to adapt to what could have been the "new her", but thank God that wasn't the case. We were in such good harmony that she even let me lay in bed with her while we watched a bunch of promo interviews for the new Marvel Infinity War movie coming out. It was genuinely one of my favorite memories to date.

A few more days of being in ICU felt like another small eternity, but thankfully all was well in this outcome. Her brain was not nearly as damaged as perceived and the seizures had since stopped. There was also no positive signs of future episodes. That following week, Alexa was transferred back to begin her new cycle of treatment.

I don't know if Alexa was more excited to be back to her normal room or if the nurses were more excited for her return. They all were awaiting her and were floored with the quick progress she made after having two seemingly detrimental seizures. Both Lex and the nurses were ready for this next and new phase. The final treatment plan was to conduct the spinal taps to ensure that the chemo was being projected directly into her spine and could disperse accordingly. It all needed start immediately. Anymore delays than she already had and the cancer could spread even quicker. Due to her incredible track record thus far, she didn't have much going for her. Our only question following approval of the spinal taps was, "what if the taps don't work, what would be the next option?" The answer, a bone marrow transplant.

11. HELPIN' HAND

A bone marrow transplant was the last and final resource that Lex had. It was a *literal* lifeline because after it was used, there was no 'next option'. No one with this form of disease, as progressive and with as many complications as she had, ever got this far. Therefore, nobody knew what the next option would be if the transplant failed. With that in mind, the spinal taps were set to be underway for the next couple of weeks. The hope was that this seizure fiasco didn't drop her back a whole bunch.

This transplant thing sounded freaky. I'm not sure how Lex reacted to it but I took my info to the world wide web of Google. Not only did I not know what bone marrow actually was and where in the world it was located in your body, but a transplant was receiving someone else's body part and that shit sounded scary as hell. Google really didn't help much in calming my nerves. It solely gave me a better sense as to what this surgery would entail. I didn't have to wait long to get all of my and everyone else's questions answered. After the chemo talk, we all got the run down on what a transplant is and what a transplant for Alexa specifically, would endure. As the doctor continued to describe the ins and outs of the potential surgery, I forced myself to look towards my parents. I couldn't help but think about what they were pondering. Having a relative in the hospital is always tough. Having a child in the hospital seems to be worse. I couldn't digest all of this information so rapidly, but they had no choice but to force themselves to do so.

As the doctor continued, I listened to the tuned out version of what he was saying. It was all definitely something new for us to learn about collectively. I wasn't fully listening until I heard the word "sibling".

"Huh", escaped from my mouth while my eyes and ears were regaining focus.

He repeated, "the closest match for a bone marrow harvest is from a sibling".

This time, I was all ears. I forgot the boat load of questions I had initially, so I left it to my parents to interrogate such procedure. After this conversation came too an end, the doctor stepped out of the room and I followed behind him to close the door. The moment he left, the questions came flooding back. Thankfully Alexa's nurse Sue, who had become like a second mom to her while in NJ, had all the answers for me.

She thoroughly re-explained what in the hell a bone marrow transplant was and why *I* was the most suitable for this position. Thinking about it now, I don't think I was *as* confused as I was terrified. I genuinely don't know who I was more scared for, me or my sister. Whoever it was, a couple hours later, I was downstairs with my mom waiting to get a blood test done. The test determined whether or not I would be a suitable match. As I sat and waited, I was a nervous wreck. What if I wasn't a match, then what? What if I was? I would have to have surgery! Millions of thoughts rushed though my head. I didn't know how much longer I could handle any of this. It seemed to be consistent and never ending, my only motivation to "keep on" was Alexa. I found my palms becoming a sweaty mess while the nurse started tapping and thumping on the inside of my arm. She continued to search for my nonexistent veins until she could find one large enough to draw blood from. What if they couldn't find my veins during the "potential surgery"? I couldn't stop thinking about all the 'what ifs'. My mind continued to race. I felt like I was playing an ongoing round of Mario Kart. However my fears became contained once I looked at my mom. Mom's always have a calmness to them, even when they're just as stressed as you. It's the "relax everything is fine" look that allowed me to finally breath without hesitation.

I took a deep breath and looked down towards the inside of my elbow. The needle was breaking way into my skin as I winced in a subtle pain. As painless as a blood test sounds, this whole experience was new to me. I attempted to close my eyes and put on a brave face because I knew who I would be benefiting if I was a match. My palms continued to sweat as I watched the nurse change the vials every few seconds. Eight vials later and the tourniquet was finally released. I had a slight urge of relief that 'the worst' was over. However 'the worst' was definitely the waiting game we were about to endure. As soon as the band aid was placed on my arm, I was in need of knowing what the results were. Though I knew that wasn't going to be the case, I wanted to mentally prepare myself to carry the weight of quite possibly saving Alexa from this forever occurring turmoil she was in.

As soon as we got back up to Lex's room, we were immediately questioned.

"Did it hurt? What did they say? Are you a match? When will you find out?"

I sat, blankly staring at the floor while my mom answered all these seemingly difficult questions. I felt like screaming as I listened to her responses because I still couldn't even fathom that we were this far in her journey already, to the point of no more options.

The weeks were filled with more physical therapy days, more occupational work, and countless more chemo treatments. Yet again, it felt like things were looking up. This time I wasn't getting my hopes up too high though. I was constantly praying for the good days to continue and hoping for these results to come back as soon as possible. While I seemed to be excited to see if I was a match, I wasn't so sure I really was. Google didn't help with this though, it only managed to keep my on my toes. The nerves stayed high until I received *the call*.

I was a very clear and healthy match. Normally patients who are tested for such things need to go through a couple of alternative tests. The stronger the match, the greater chance of a successful transplant. Now that we knew, the next calls being made were to each and every family member to ensure them that if and when Alexa needed a transplant, I would be her harvest. These conversations were extremely difficult to have because I had to sound like I was ready for this crap to happen at any time. Though, I was anything *but* ready. Each call brought tears to my eyes. I've been practicing lying since birth, but lying about something this serious was almost impossible. As I swallowed tears of sadness, everyone else expressed tears of joy. They were over the moon excited about the news. God forbid she needed this transplant, we didn't have to go though the long process of finding someone else. Who knows how long that may have taken. It was definitely lengthy time that Alexa didn't have.

After I finally processed this knowledge, I did a crazy amount of thinking. Although this still *sounded* like something from a movie, it also felt too real at the same time. I was obviously going to go though with the surgery out of guilt, but if and when the time came, I didn't want to feel guilty. I wanted to be of help to my sister in any way possible but I was scared of helping in such a way. In hope that I would be able to go into the surgery without guilt riding on my shoulders, I did a ton of soul searching. As dumb as it sounds, it was genuinely what I needed.

I went to school and did my schoolwork, worked almost everyday, continued to see my mom and Alexa on the weekends, and continued with all my other responsibilities. However one thing was added to that list, I spoke. While I was alone in my car driving to or from wherever I was going at that moment, I spoke to both God and my grandma. While I'm sure they were both caught up and even ahead of what I was thinking and feeling, I needed to have them hear it from me.

The first time I spoke to them was when I was leaving my grandpas house and on my way to work at Party City. As I opened the door and sat down, I instantly broke down. If you know me, you know that I rarely *ever* cry. In situations where one would normally cry, I laugh. But this time, it was no laughing matter. I couldn't help *but* cry. As I backed out of the driveway and drove up the block, I felt the need to pull over. My glasses were filled with tears and my face had streams of black mascara coming from every way possible. Not the look I was going for that afternoon. I remember this moment so vividly because it was the moment I *finally* turned to someone else for help. My entire life, as you can tell, I've done or tried to do everything myself. Whenever I feel some type of emotions come up, I try my best to suppress them and put my best foot forward. My grandma always taught me that if I wanted something done to do it myself, but this time, it felt like I reached my peak of "doing it myself". I sat, cried, and wished that there was someone that I could talk too. I didn't need to have them respond, just listen. While a tear streamed down my face and the clock continued to wind down to my shift beginning, I remembered them. I *did* have people to talk to who would solely listen to me, my grandma, and God, all I needed.

My grandma was my absolute best friend in the whole wide world. Growing up, I wanted to be nothing less than who she was as not only an individual, but as a mom, wife, grandma, sister and so much more. She was the epitome of incredible. She did her absolute best for everyone at any time. Working her ass off for her family was her greatest talent. The way she loved and cared for people, even if she just met or didn't know them, was my favorite quality of hers. She opened her door to anyone so they could feel at home. An extra bonus was that she knew just about everything there was to know in this world. Anyone that had the opportunity of knowing her could attest to that. So who better to turn to than her. With that, I started the car, wiped the tears from my eyes and began to drive and talk.

I told her everything! I talked about how I felt when I first heard the news about Alexa being diagnosed, all the way up until now with this damn transplant.

I cried the entire way through. I've been holding my feelings and emotions in for so long that it felt so good to let it out, knowing that no one was going to be crying back to me. The normal drive to work would have taken about 20 minutes but the traffic and constant stopping to wipe the fog on my glasses from crying managed to make it an hour long trip. Although I know I was undoubtedly about an hour and a half late for work, I didn't care. I really needed that time, that cry, that talk. I needed it all. That hour journey was clearly filled with tears but not necessarily sad tears. They were tears of relief. The entire evening at work consisted of me reflecting on what the fuck happened on the drive. I continued to ask myself the dreaded question, "What would happen if I said no to doing the transplant?" Now each time I asked this question, I didn't feel guilty saying "No". I was no longer scared of the idea of having surgery nor was I feeling unprepared for such an event to happen in my life. For someone who fears just about anything and everything that the world has to offer, that says a lot. However, I was no longer on edge and the amount of relief I felt from that day forward was immaculate. On days where I wanted to feel that same kind of self acceptance, I knew who to turn too.

12. FIGHT SONG

The third week of July came around real quick. The countless prayers, love and wishes were serving us right for the first time in forever. Alexa's second set of chemo sessions were finally coming to an end. From then on she would be receiving a new form of chemo in addition to radiation. This time though, she didn't technically need to be an inpatient to receive both of them. Therefore, there was a possible transfer date back to New York approaching us real soon... with a catch of course.

As she was close to finishing up her final days of chemo, we were even closer to finding out when she was able to go home. However the catch was that after she concluded her treatment, she needed a week of being in near perfect health in just about every aspect. Her counts had to be up, her sicknesses had to subside, and her temperature couldn't fluctuate. If she contracted any type of infection throughout that week, she would be dropped back to day one and the process would start all over again.

During the first few days, everything was going well. Her counts were considerably high for how low they've been thus far. She was thankfully not feeling any signs of sickness, just the occasional tired from being on so many meds. Throughout that week, she was able to continue her physical therapy here and there which revealed the strength that she was now feeling. She was doing outstandingly well. Her progress gave us hope and hope brought us a transfer date! The date was July 20th. The reaction on everyone's face and the excitement in their voices is something that I will forever remember. No one believed the day would actually come! We've been going down this road for so long, it felt like a dead end. When I walked into Alexa's room the following weekend, she had the biggest smile on her face. The months upon months of hell that she endured, she was finally going to have freedom! That smile shined brighter than ever.

As the days were winding down to the 20th, Alexa's doctor came to follow up with her before her final days there. Although she was doing extremely well, they wanted to give her a vaccine before she was able to leave. It was a shot that would boost her immune system. Being in the hospital and constantly getting transfusions and fluids whenever needed, she had no build up of an immune system. Therefore, when she goes outside for the first time and breathes the air from the ever so clean world around her, they didn't want it to knock her off her feet. However, the shot couldn't be delivered to the hospital, it had to be delivered to a home. The closest house to RWJ was Sesa's house. She gave the doctor Sesa's address and waited for the set back to come around the corner. The vaccine would take up to a week to be delivered. So the magical "home date" that was within her reach was now disappearing into thin air.

When I called my mom that night she told me the dreaded news. I didn't even want to know how Alexa was feeling because I'm sure she was as pissed off as the rest of us. She was so damn close that we could practically taste it. The hope that she was finally going home was ripped from her. Hopefully it was only a few more days but anything other than the 20th was just sad. As I talked and attempted to reassure her, I was praying that she would stay in good health all while waiting for this vaccine.

This was the first time I didn't want to go see her on the weekend because I was not up to seeing the disappointment on her face. She made this journey look effortless, even though she had gone through more shit in a few months than most people go through in a lifetime. I couldn't stand to see how miserable she was going to be at something that was yet again, out of her control. She was doing so incredibly well with learning how to walk and getting back on her feet, that I didn't want this minor setback to seem major to her. I still went to see her that weekend in hope of putting a smile on her face.

On the car ride there, my dad and I talked about how we could possibly cheer her up. Alexa tried her best to stay positive about everything. Her philosophy of everything that happened to her in the past few months was that "God only chooses battles for people that could handle and overcome them". After a constant battle for almost 9 months, I was afraid she was just about gassed out. On the elevator ride up, I was nervous about looking into her eyes and trying to convince her that the vaccine was coming soon and that she would be home in no time. It seemed like everything that everyone "knew" was always false.

When I opened the door, my jaw dropped. Alexa was standing straight up, holding onto her walker. I looked at my moms face and watched her smile grow bigger and bigger. I looked at Alexa's face when she turned her head and looked back at my dad and I.

"Hey Dee. Hey Dad."

I never felt the need to happy cry more in my entire life than in that moment. To see that the determination was still on her face after she was told "No" (you can't leave yet), is something that sticks with me everyday. I walked around her bed to give her and my mom a kiss while my jaw followed behind me. Not only have I not seen Alexa get up by herself in a long while, I also have *never* seen her not only feeling but looking like herself again. In that moment I really didn't care that the vaccine hadn't come yet, all I cared about were the smiles. We haven't smiled like that as a family in such a long time.

Later that afternoon, Sesa came to pick me up. Lex was telling her all about her standing up again and walking. She was determined to do so again tomorrow; this time the entire floor. She was so excited to finally walk again and she wanted us all to attend. Sesa pinky promised that we would all be right behind her.

I played music in the car as we were driving home. Since before Alexa was diagnosed, both her and Sesa would sing the 'Fight Song' by Rachel Platten at the top of their lungs whenever it came on the radio. After she was diagnosed, the meaning behind the song changed. It was still a bop of course but now the fight was more of a fight to continue being strong and waking up every day as oppose to a fight with me or the boys. I played that song as a joke to see if Sesa would cry, but in the end, both of us were in a puddle of tears. Although sometimes things seemed down, the warrior of a sister I had wouldn't allow it. She was fighting and so were we, each and every damn day. It was a moment that I will never forget. Not only was it the first time I've cried in a while, but Sesa and I connected in a way we never had before, an emotional connection. That song made us feel empowered and made us appreciate and remember how far Alexa had come. We needed to remind ourselves how lucky we are to have such a badass fighter in the family.

That following morning we all woke up and headed straight to the hospital. Chris, Nicky, and I were listening to music while Sesa drove. All I was thinking about was watching Alexa walk again. It was Friday, July 20th, the day that she was supposed to come home. Knowing that today was *the* day, I was feeling sad and hopeful. I tried to push the sad out of the way and focus on today, the hopeful.

She was as healthy as she's ever been since being in any hospital. She was pushing harder than ever to stay motivated. God's willing, that vaccine would soon show up in Rutherford, NJ and she would be coming home for good! As we pulled up to RWJ, the boys and I raced up to the front door. We walked in with the attempt of being as civil as possible and checked in together. We gunned it to her door to see a smiley Alexa. She had her shoes on and was ready to run around the nurse's station. We patiently waited for one of her nurses to assist her in getting up and putting her seatbelt on. Within the blink of an eye she was buckled up and ready to go. Her nurse walked right next to her with her IV stand in hand. We all attempted to follow behind them but they were a bit speedy if I do say so myself. Boy was this girl getting fast. You would've never even guessed that she was ever fully immobile at one point. She was like Lighting damn McQueen on that hospital floor. As she walked around the circle all the nurses were cheering her on.

Although I never told Alexa how much she inspired me, I not so secretly always wanted to be like her. This kind of inspiration was something I've never seen. Her eyes were screaming "I can do it" and I had no doubt she couldn't. I finally agreed with the fact that however long the vaccine took to arrive, it was going to be a piece of cake for her. She shut my nervous ass up real quick as soon as I walked in the door. She had a newfound strength and she was striving for the finish line.

Each day Sesa called and updated me about the shot. Since I left her house of the 21st, I've been waiting for the "it's here!" phone call but the days passed and I had yet to receive it. It felt draining for all of us because we wanted her home so terribly. At least I knew that she was keeping her head up and I was going to try my best to do the same.

On the evening of July 30th, Sesa checked the mail on her front doorstep. To her surprise, there it was! The white box containing the key to bringing Alexa back home.

"I got the goods" she screamed as she called my mom and Lex. "I'm heading over now!"

I received the call next and from then, I passed on the news around to everyone. Alexa was finally, positively, coming home! As the evening fell, Sesa pulled up to RWJ. She practically flew there because she was so excited. Alexa's nurse injected it into her and began the paperwork to send her home the following day. Thinking about it now, it felt like this day would never come, but tomorrow the second part of this journey came to a conclusion. The in-patient hospital days were over! Home, here she comes!

The following morning was the big day! It was the day Alexa has been awaiting for what felt like years. It was July 31, 2018 and New York was in her near future. Sesa was the chosen one to take Alexa and my mom home from the hospital. Before the re-entrance to life, they had to make one more pitstop at Cohens to situate her plans for her new schedule of radiation.

When they finally arrived at the front door, my mom had a question lingering in her head since before they left. Where would Alexa stay? She had yet to attempt stairs, so she couldn't stay at our house in Jackson Heights because our room was on the second floor. My grandpa's house seemed to be the only viable option. At the same time, we didn't want to disturb him by practically moving in, all four of our lives into his home. Although, we've been *technically* living there since birth. However the moment he heard the crazy talk, he was beyond willing to give up the entire house for Alexa. With that being said, plans were quickly arranged for the four of us.

The excitement I felt and expressed when I walked in the door and saw my sister laying on the couch was extremely memorable. I have genuinely never been so happy to see her in my entire life. First, she was breathing oxygen that wasn't contaminated with hospital. Second, she was at our grandmas house, which if you ask me is the best place to be. Third, both Nanny and Grandpa who haven't seen Alexa or heard her voice in months, were finally able to spend some time with her. It genuinely felt like the whole world went back to normal when I saw her that day. Even though things weren't perfect just yet, I felt a sense of comfort that I hadn't felt in a long time. Finally, our happy family back together again with my guardian angel grandma looking over us all.

13. ONTO THE NEXT

As quick as the first night went, the morning rolled around it it was another day in the office for Alexa. She was up when I was getting ready for school and out the door while I was having breakfast. She started the day with a 5am medicine. From then on she was getting ready for her first day back at the hospital. This time, she was an out patient!

When I came home from school that day, I was greeted by Alexa sobbing on the couch watching "This is Us", just a casual day in the Roberto household. I tossed my backpack by the wall and hugged her. I started doing my homework while I listened to Lex continuing to sob over a Netflix show. While I was working, my mom was telling me all about her first radiation session. Every other day Lex was scheduled to have radiation followed by a check up of her counts. It consisted of a finger prick which allowed the nurses to know if she needed blood or platelets. If she needed a transfusion, she would head over to the out patient clinic where she would fuel up with whatever she needed. Alexa would stay there for a couple of hours and then be free to go home. It wasn't a bad gig compared to the hell she had gone through prior. Home was the goal and she already accomplished that.

The first two weeks of Alexa's radiation sessions passed and when I got home each day, I would see her knocked out on the couch. This shit really hit her hard. As hard as she was pushing to become stronger each and every day, the effects of what she had and what she was continuing to go through was starting to show, but it wasn't stopping her. Just a small afternoon nap when she came home and she ready to continue the day. However, the following week was a bit different. As I plowed through the front door yelling "hunnies I'm home", I felt the difference all the way from the kitchen. I got no reaction to my loud mouth self. I propped my bag down on the floor and gave my mom a hug and kiss.

"You're gonna have to have the transplant".

The topic of conversation at dinner was none other than… the transplant. As my brain registered what she said, I responded with "okay, cool". But 'okay, cool' was not what was going through my head. I was for sure in full panic mode! That night, dinner felt like a hazy nightmare. As we all sat down at the dinner table, my mom talked and talked and talked. I casually listened to not a word, so nothing short from the usual. When I finally decided to concentrate and leave the world my mind was in, she was enlightening everyone on how the radiation treatment wasn't working as well as they had hoped. The cancer was not necessarily spreading at the moment, but the 'dosage' they were giving her was all her body could handle. They couldn't up the dosage to something that was already not fully working. The cancer cells would simply get used to the poison trying to kill them and come back stronger and potentially in a different form. It could cause a potential spread. Now for the new idea, the bone marrow transplant. I still didn't quite understand this whole concept even though its been explained to me countless times. All I knew was that the following day I would be going to the hospital to have a few tests done.

I woke up to my heart racing and practically beating out of my chest. My palms were sweating already and all I did thus far was roll over in bed and scroll through Instagram and Snapchat. I looked up from my phone to see both my mom and Lex watching TV. Today was the start to MY journey. The journey to hopefully being able to save my sisters life.

Although my wake up wasn't ideal, the moment I saw Alexa's face, I was cured. I knew she was going to be with me every step of the way. She was a pro at this point and although I knew the day was going to be anything but normal, I was ready. I figured that Alexa had an abrupt start to her journey but she managed to mend well with all the changes. The only difference between us is that she's okay with change. Me, not so much. I'm not a strong advocate for such "changes". It's probably one of my least favorite things in the world. So, while I knew it wasn't going to be smooth sailing, I needed to remain positive because I yearned for the normalcy of life back, as I'm sure everyone else did as well. With this going through my mind, we heard a honk outside. To Cohens we went.

All we did was talk on the ride there. Lex told me step by step what was going to happen and I was definitely listening this time. Although I knew nothing terrible was going to happen to me, I knew pain was inevitable, missing school was hopefully not in my future, and I was praying that I wasn't going to have to stay overnight in the hospital. As we pulled up to one of the buildings, the driver hopped out of the car and slide open our door. My mom and I stepped out and walked around to the back of the car to wait for Lex. He opened the back doors, unbuckled Alexa's seatbelt and wheeled her onto the curb. Our first stop was Alexa's radiation treatment which was located in a different building attached to the hospital. Lex led the way as my mom pushed her wheelchair and listened to her firm direction telling. I walked behind them with the upmost confusion as to where the hell we were going. We walked in the door and took a ride up the elevator to meet with two of the happiest people I've ever met at 8am. They were bubbly as can be with huge bright smiles across their faces. They greeted us like they've known us forever. The nurses walked both my mom and I to our waiting room while Alexa was wheeled off to begin her treatment. I *attempted* to do homework while my mom was peacefully resting in the chair across from me. About an hour later Alexa was finished and we were then headed off to the main building. I knew the way this time so I led. As we approached the sliding doors to the front of Cohens Children Specialized Hospital, it was bittersweet to say the least. Not having come here the past couple of months while Lex was in NJ making constant progress made me realize how much Cohens helped her in the beginning of her diagnosis. A large majority of her journey thus far was spent at Cohens, getting somewhat adherent to life again. Now it was my turn to spend a bit of time here as well. I rolled Alexa to the front desk where we got out visitors stickers and she then told me where my first appointment was going to be. It was on the first floor right behind the check in desk. It was across from the resource center that her and my mom would normally sit at in-between radiation sessions. She worked on my college apps there so I could hopefully be somewhat successful in getting into college.

We checked into my appointment and waited to get called in. It was around 11 am and we were the second family there. My heart plummeted to my toes when I heard my name being called. I walked in behind the nurse while my mom and Alexa trailed on my heels. She took my blood pressure and asked me a few questions about my families medical history.

Within a few breaths, the doctor pranced into the room. She began looking at my chart and asking even more questions. At one point, she asked both my mom and Alexa if they could step out of the room. Her following questions were sex based and "were to stay between her and I". Though after constant head shakes 'No' and awkward laughs, I walked out of the room and reunited with my family in the waiting room. One appointment down and one remaining. The first one wasn't too bad so I was feeling a bit more mellow than I was when I walked in. I went into the second appointment with an open mind and a slight headache from not eating this morning.

My second and final appointment for the day was on the fourth floor. I walked in and wrote my name down on the patient check in paper and sat down. Being the children that my sister and I are, we gunned it to the toys that we spotted in the middle of the room. I could see the tiredness coming through Lex's eyes but I didn't mention it. I just soaked up the sister sister time. We continued to play Pictionary and Scrabble on the tablet inspired table that was in front of us. Soon one of the nurses opened the door and called, "Deanna Roberto". I stood up with a slight hesitation as if the name she called wasn't me. As I walked into the room containing everything screaming blood test, I knew I was going to be the next victim.

"Did you eat anything this morning?" the nurse said. I nodded my head in approval but that couldn't be further from the truth. Oh well. My fingers just happened to stay crossed in hope I didn't pass out. As she was prepping the needle and all my vials, another nurse walked in and introduced herself to me. Her name was the same as my grandmas and suddenly all my fears vanished. She was the flibotamist that was going to take my blood and so she continued prepping me with alcohol swabs. I gave her the brief heads up about my nonexistent veins like I do with everyone but she said,

"Don't worry, it'll be okay."

Within a few seconds of tapping and pressing on the inside of my arm, she began inserting the needle. I was ready for a shock of pain but I didn't feel a damn thing. As she began switching the vials after they filled up, I was slowly started to convince myself that I was getting lightheaded, just casual hypochondriac things. Once she said, "we're finished", I was ready for the worst pain, the needle being pulled out. Yet again, no pain. I was floored to say the least. I quickly got up from the chair and followed the nurse into the next room. I was accompanied by the two psychos who let me take that (not so) scary blood test alone.

As I propped myself onto the bed, I sat as patiently as possible. My mom and Alexa were looking at me as I told them all about the flibotamist and how she didn't hurt me at all. My story got cut short when the door swung open and I met the bone marrow transplant social worker. She introduced herself and assured me that she had been apart of Alexa's case since the beginning. My nerves lessened even more. This day wasn't going as horribly as I perceived after all. She basically gave me a break down of everything that would happen the day of the transplant. I got prepped for before and after the procedure. I soaked up as much information as I possibly could but I knew I had four backup ears listening as well. As the conversation came to end, she asked if I had any questions about such procedure.

"Not about the procedure but about school. Is there any way that we can schedule it so that I don't miss a day of school because I've had perfect attendance for almost my entire high school career."

I never thought that *that* was the question that would come to my mind after just finding out that a syringe would be injected into the bottom of my back as a wine side bottle of bone marrow would be taken from me. But here I was, worried about school! Those talks with God and my grandma helped a shit ton, geez.

She responded with, "I'll try my best too but if not, I'll send a note to your principal and hopefully they'll excuse the absence."

I didn't love that response but I looked at Alexa who looked back at me and nodded. So, I mimicked her action. With that, we were off to contact the oncology social worker to get us a ride back home!

14. THE NEWS HEARD ROUND THE WORLD

Alexa's social worker was an angel above all. Throughout her time at Cohens, she helped us immensely. We would not have gotten very far without her. Between questions, concerns, transportation, and so much more, she did it all.

When we returned home that day, we were exhausted. We collectively called it an early night after dinner and knocked the hell out out in my grandpas bed.

The realization that I would have to have weekly blood tests to ensure that my counts stayed high and I stayed healthy took me aback for a second, but I was prepared. I went to school the following morning and headed straight to the principals office. I asked if it was possible to be excused the day of the surgery. However, the response I received was heart shattering. While that *does* sounds a bit dramatic, it was kind of rough hearing that the years of prefect attendance were easily going to get thrown down the drain. Perfect attendance was within my reach until I found out about the surgery. Though I still had some hope that my bone marrow social worker's letter was going to come in handy. I was hoping she could sway the rules but in the back of my head I knew it was still a definitive no. My final leap of faith was having the transplant scheduled on the Monday that we were off for the Veterans Day holiday.

While the final date was still up in the air, I somehow managed to still be ill prepared. I was mentally there but I still needed a kick in the ass to be fully *there*. While my family gave me the hope I needed, I yearned for a positive push from the people in the place that I attended everyday. I began telling teachers that Alexa and I became close with over the years.

First, I went to Mrs. Flynn who had been Alexa's buddy since she started at TMLA. She was so proud of me for agreeing without hesitation.

She assured me that I was doing the best thing for Alexa and her health. Next, I went to Mrs. Rezin, who quickly became a second mom to the both of us. She was Alexa's senior year Anatomy teacher. I got to know her very well during that time and she easily became a confidant to me. As I told her about the news, she began to cry. She expressed to me how grateful Alexa was going to be because *I* was having this surgery. Finally, I took a trip to the convent in our campus and walked up the stairs to Ms. Sama's office. Ms. Sama was the glue that kept me together. I talked to her about anything and everything, wether it was about Alexa and I's situation or not. Everyone else, including advisors, teachers, and friends found out somewhere along the lines. With such news being so public now, I felt a bit of pressure to stay in exemplary health to ensure that the surgery would be as close to success as possible. However, at the same time I was beginning to rediscover the nerves that I tried so hard to fight off.

During the following weeks, I continued my blood test examinations. Each week provided the same news I thankfully continued to be in great health. Finally, something was going right! Alexa's doctors were getting prepared to schedule the harvest date. That's when everything really became full circle. Of course it was all real, but it still seemed so hard to believe. The whole situation continued to feel like a dream in disguise. When I finally received the harvest date, I swallowed the fact that this shit was tangible and it was all going down in two weeks. October 15th 2018 was the day!

Each day leading up to the transplant day was nerve wrecking. I wasn't so much scared anymore as I was wildly nervous. I've never really been put under anesthesia other than the one time I had an endoscopy when I was about 11. I've never been apart of anything "medical-ish" other than that. So, a first time *real* procedure was definitely playing with my mind a bunch. Each day when I went to school, I often took it Ms. Sama's couch and told her bout my thoughts. She was always down to listen to all the crazy shit coming out of my mouth.

October 14th came within the blink of an eye. All day, I was wishing that time went faster so I could be done with this procedure already. That evening I had some tasks to do and by I, I mean my mom. We had to clean the surface of my back that was going to be worked on the following day with a bunch of medical surgery stuff. While my mom cleaned my back with the saturated cloth after my nighttime shower, I laid in bed and fell right asleep. That was the most restless night of sleep I ever had. Thank God I was being put back to sleep in just a couple hours. I woke up that morning at 5:30 and headed straight to the fridge to get some orange juice. I stopped in my tracks when I realized I couldn't eat or drink anything before the procedure. While I stomped down the hall in anger and climbed back into bed, I looked around in the dark for the clothes I had set out the night before. I traced each part of the bed with my palm until I found the sweatpants and hoodie I put out, a navy blue hoodie that matched my Maritime sweats. It was all going to come off as soon as I played dress up in the hospital and changed into my beautifully patterned gown with grey socks. I was surely about be runway ready in no time. By 6:30, my dad and I were on the road to what felt like ongoing hell. As we pulled up to the front doors, my mom met me at the entrance and walked me towards the check-in area. We had to fill out a bunch of papers and get my ID and insurance checked before we could even travel into the waiting area. I was getting confused in the system with my sister of course, because why not. About an hour later all my problems were solved and we were rounding the corner towards the elevator to proceed downstairs. As we were walking past the screen doors, I glimpsed at the parking lot outside and saw Soraya, Dayanara, and my Aunt Val all walking in unison towards the entrance. While seeing them walk towards me didn't surprise me because I knew they wouldn't miss wishing me good luck for the world, I was surprised at the fact that I instantly became more anxious when I saw them because I knew that time was running out. As we all walked in an assembly line to the waiting room, we sat and waited pensively. The energy that was being radiated throughout the room included silence, humor, and nervousness all at once. Then, the door opened.

"Deanna Roberto" the woman in scrubs called out.

I got up and walked to the door with my mom a few paces behind me. We were walking to the pre-operation room which was the last place I would be in before the procedure room. As the nurse swung open the curtain, in front of me stood a hospital bed lined with two gowns and a pair of no slip hospital socks. To the right of the bed was the dreaded beeping machine that I hated oh so much. Within minutes of hopping onto the bed, I had an IV placed into my hand and I was engulfed in hospital gear from head to toe. I tried my best to act as normal as possible while everyone gradually took turns coming in and wishing me good luck. As time continued to wind down, the anesthesiologist was the next to visit to introduce herself and go over protocol. Interacting with someone who was going to be present in the room during the procedure made me feel a tad bit more comfortable. After a few more family visits and a couple more times of my mom telling me that I couldn't wear sweats into the operating room, the nurse technicians burst through the double doors. I finally had no choice but to slide out of my Maritime sweats and hand my glasses over to my mom. My blind ass walked hand in hand with the nurses and rounded the corner into another room. I unfortunately remember *everything* from that moment on.

The room was bright and white. Machines of all shapes and sizes covered the entirety of the floor. There were four people waiting for my arrival besides the woman who opened the door and the one holding my hand. There were two other nurses, the anesthesiologist and the doctor that was present in the room. I was instructed to sit onto of the long linen lined table and lay down on my back. As I proceeded to do so, the anesthesiologist informed me that I may begin to feel drowsy because she was inserting a dosage of anesthesia into my IV as we spoke. I felt my eyes begin to get heavy, though I'm sure that was just me forcing myself to go to sleep. I figured the sooner I got to sleep, the sooner I would wake up and it would all be over. Within a few minutes passing, I was positive I was forcing myself to sleep because I was well into already receiving my second dosage of anesthesia and nothing was happening.

"So the anesthesia doesn't seem to be enough for you. I'm gonna put a mask on you that is going to circulate laughing gas. You're just gonna inhale and exhale like normal. It's okay to laugh so don't worry if you do. Just relax and breathe."

As she placed the mask on me, I slowly inhaled and exhaled a few times. My world felt like it was shifting. I was experiencing the weirdest and worst feeling that I have ever felt in my entire life. It felt as if there was an elephant sitting on my chest. From the neck down my body was numb. I didn't know what exactly was happening but I attempted to keep my focus on my breathing. As I continued to respire, I began searching for the linen drop sheet that I was laying on with my hands. Although my hands felt like they had pins and needles, I felt that as long as I could grab onto something and somewhat move my hands, I was fine. The first thought that ran into my looney toon brain was that I was paralyzed. I'm not sure how I came to such conclusion simply through inhaling this laced oxygen, but I managed to get there. As I continued my scavenger hunt, I finally felt the fabric at my fingertips. I clenched it in my fists and instantly felt more calm because at least I knew I wasn't paralyzed. However, I still felt this thousand pound weight on my chest. I figured if I didn't survive this intoxicated oxygen, I at least had everyone I loved waiting outside for me. So, I continued to breath as peacefully as possible.

"Okay, she's asleep." I vividly remember hearing those exact words come from the anesthesiologists' mouth.

I tried everything in my power to open my eyes but I couldn't. I tried to open my mouth to talk but I couldn't. I tried to shake my head as if to signal that I was clearly not asleep just yet, but I couldn't. I was frozen and numb. I tried my best to stay calm but I was as close to a full blown panic attack as ever. I was completely able to hear through half of the procedure until I the anesthesia kicked my ass and took my hearing powers away. I thankfully drifted off so the next time I opened my eyes, I was in a new room, the post-operation room. I woke up to the sight of both of my parents looking up at a small TV in my room. Playing on it was a black and white cowboy show that my dad and grandpa watch every Sunday on MeTV. As I looked down, I saw the pulsator warped around my pointer finger, an IV still in its place in my arm, and a cuff hooking me up to the pressure machine. I felt a tight pull from what I imagined was the bandage squeezing at my sides. I shifted my body to get a bit more comfortable in this seemingly already uncomfortable situation. As I moved, I felt my whole body shift to one side and I let out a slight yelp of pain. My parents swung their heads around. My mom came to my bedside and my dad looked right back up at the TV. He couldn't miss the *new* episode of the 1950s cowboy show!

"Don't move. They're gonna come to change your bandages in a little bit, cook" my mom said as she patted my hand. "I gotta go back upstairs to your sister because she's been asking for me but your father is gonna stay here. Right, Lou? Lou. LOU!"

"Yeah. Yeah. I'm here."

My dad hated being in the hospital or in the presence of any doctor *ever*. He's a gentle soul with a not so gentle build. If you see him walking down the street, you might choose to walk the opposite direction in hope to not pass this massive Hulk man. When Alexa and I were babies, he was nervous to pick us up because he was afraid he was going to crush us. So hospital, plus not one but two children present and being "worked on" was not his most astounding moment of parenthood as one could assume.

A nurse swooped in to my post-opt room and asked me how I was doing. I was feeling okay, just a little achy but not necessarily in pain. I had a headache the size of Texas but I figured it came with the anesthesia wearing off. I was also pretty sure my back was either bleeding or I had peed on myself. She walked around me, checking my vitals and such as I continued to tell her how I was feeling.

"I'm gonna check the dressing and the bandages that they put on after the procedure. I'm gonna see if they need to be changed now or if we can wait a bit."

As I shook my head yes, I watched my dad bounce out of his chair and rushed over to me. She asked me to slowly roll over so she can see the wound. He grabbed my hand that was reaching over to the left in hope to reach the stretcher bar that I didn't quite make. As I turned to my side, I felt the puddle of what I was now sure was blood, drip down my back.

"Wow! Okay, so I'm actually gonna go get everything to change the dressings and bandages now."

My dad spoke for me this time as I squealed in pain. "Okay, sounds good."

Our hands remained clutched as I stayed turned on my hip until the nurse returned to us with the wound care. I felt her touch my back and begin to peel off the saturated bandages. I immediately felt sore as the air quickly clung to the hole that was now present in my back. The nurse described each thing that she was doing as it was being done. A few minutes later, I was wrapped up like a sausage again. As I turned to lay on my back again, I felt the room begin to spin. I didn't appreciate that one bit. Being nauseous, throwing up, and being dizzy were all things that I could happily go on without ever having to experience. They were the absolute worst.

As the anesthesia continued to wear off, I closed my eyes and slept for another two hours. I was hoping that the sleep would make the nausea go away so that I would be able to get up and walk the hell out of here. I ain't no superwoman though, so that didn't work. When I woke up again, I attempted to sit up and swing my legs to the side so my feet were dangling. I managed to pick my head up off the pillow and stretch my neck upwards before I felt lightheaded. My dad rushed up to me to ask if I wanted something to drink so that I could get something in my system to hopefully feel less dizzy. As the nurse heard that I wanted to try to drink something, she sprinted over with drink options. I chose the red Gatorade. It reminded me of what my mom used to give my sister and I anytime we were sick growing up. It seemed to fit the mood just right. I also figured the electrolytes would give me some type of energy. At least I hoped it did because I was already there for way longer than I anticipated. It did the exact opposite. I fell asleep again. This time when I woke up, my mom was present, standing right next too my dad. She told me that I had to walk and use the restroom before I was allowed to leave the post-opt room. After that, I was free to head upstairs to Lex's room.

"Everyone is waiting for you upstairs because Lex has something to give you."

"What is it?" my impatient ass asked.

"I don't know. Drink some more Gatorade so your head can feel better."

I gave her the eyebrow raise and sipped my Gatorade can like it was presented to me in a teacup, pinky up and all. The next hour went by and I tried to get up again. I was slightly less dizzy but still felt the nausea getting to me as I continued my journey to my feet. I fell back down on my elbow even though I tried my best to stay as propped up as possible. I was determined to get up. I simply closed my eyes and forced myself to not feel the nausea. I continued to sit up an inch more each time my stomach and head had settled. I quickly found myself looking straight at the curtain that was on my right. As I opened my eyes, my mom and dad both came to my bedside.

"Are you ready to try to get up or do you wanna wait a little longer."

"I'm good. I'm good. I'm gonna get up in a minute" I said as I chugged some more gatorade.

I waited another few minutes until my curiosity of what was waiting for me upstairs got the best of me.

"I'm ready. Can y'all help me up."

I waited for my mom and the nurse to come to my bedsides so I could make my attempt at standing. As I slowly pointed my left toe down to find the floor, I pulled on both of their arms to force my body upright. I felt so faint it was as if a gust of wind could take me out. I stood for a moment with my eyes closed before deciding to take any steps. When I finally started moving, I was on the run. I headed to the bathroom first and then back to the bed to rip that gown off and put my comfy clothes back on. I wasn't focused on the pain anymore, I just wanted to know what my surprise was. The moment I slipped my hoodie back on I was buzzing to have the nurse come back to see if I was all clear to head upstairs.

"I need to call for a wheelchair to take you upstairs because you're not allowed to walk by yourself just yet. If you're ready, I'll call one now."

"Yes please. I'm ready", I said with the biggest smile on my face.

She nodded her head and grinned as she walked off. As I turned my attention to the Disney channel show that was playing on my TV, I couldn't help but overhear a conversation that was happening in the next room over. I concluded that the male teenager next to me was as nervous as ever for his first surgery. So nervous that he wasn't sure if the procedure had happened yet. The nerves were of course getting the best of him and I felt terrible. When one of the nurses came in to check my vitals before leaving, she knew I was eavesdropping and filled a girl in with some important information; he was super cute. From that moment on, I was prepping for my slow drive (in my wheelchair) past his room. I was trying my absolute best to lift my hands up high enough to fix my messy ass hair. When I finally wrangled up all my baby hairs into one messy bun, the nurse was strolling in with my wheelchair. It was my time to shine! I waddled my way over and propped myself up as nice and pretty as possible. I braced myself to glance over at this attractive boy and look semi human while doing so. At this point the surprise had left my mind for a hot second. As I was slowly wheeled past the next room, I looked up and with the utmost confidence in my voice and told him that he would be just fine. It was all I could mutter out of my mouth because the nurse was right, he was hot. Him and his parents giggled and thanked me. I was pretty sure I just fell in love but the moment had quickly passed when we got to the elevator and were seconds away from seeing Alexa.

As the elevator doors opened, my mom walked in front of us to guide us all up to her room. She rang the bell to get buzzed in and we were greeted with nothing but smiles from everyone. As per usual, everyone knew my mom by name and I was yet again assumed to be Alexa's sister. Never gets old, huh. As the nurse came from behind me to help me up, my mom and dad were getting all spiffied up to enter Alexa's room. It took me a little while to get my gloves, gown, and mask on because I couldn't quite see straight but I was not about to sit back down in that damn wheelchair. I couldn't seem like I was in an immense amount of pain because I was about to see Lex, the girl who has gone through hell and back in just a few short months. I also know if I seemed weak it was going to make her feel worse than she already did. When I finally managed to slip both gloves on and dress to impress, we were ready to go inside. My mom opened the door and stepped in first as I followed. I looked around at the crowd of family members staring at me. I was quick to notice that there wasn't a dry eye in the house. The one time I didn't want to be center of attention was in this moment but it was in fact, all eyes on me.

I got up as quick as I could and walked over to sit on Alexa's bed. I was walking like an 90 year old man, crunched over and as slow as molasses. I couldn't quite put a finger on why everyone was crying simultaneously but at this point, my focus was on Alexa and the giant blue bag that was on her lap.

"What's that?" I asked with a devilish grin on my face.

"Remember that expensive gift I could get because of the transplant." I nodded my head and winced in pain all at once. "Well, I used it on you." Tears began flooding from her eyes as well.

I will never forget the look she gave me in that moment. It wasn't solely tears of sorrow or tears of pain, they were tears of thanks. "Thank you for helping me. I'm sorry you're in pain but thank you for doing it for me. I love you" she said as she wiped the tears away.

She slid over the bag from her lap onto mine. I unzipped it and looked all the way down to the bottomless pit of happiness. It was like little rays of sunshine were beaming out from the inside. My eyes were peeled and my mouth was gaped open. I pulled out one thing at a time. First multiple sketchbook with all different kinds of paper. Then, Blick markers, Prismacolor pencils, and a ton more art supplies. I couldn't even begin to express my thanks, I was too busy taking it all in.

Alexa is the most selfless person I've ever met. I was for sure she was going to donate the money like she said she wanted to. Although I made fun of her at the time, I believe I would have done the same thing. Being in a situation like hers, it was hard to imagine that there were others that were in the same or even in a predicament than Lex. Donating the money gave us a fresh mindset and appreciation for what she *has* and the health that she is fighting so hard to regain. Going along with this transplant, although it was touch and go in my head at times, I would've never disagreed to it. I didn't want or expect any appreciation or party after it was over. I just wanted my sister to get better so she can finally go and stay home. However, the fact that she chose to use the money she was given to thank *me* because she couldn't get or do much otherwise, sent tears to my eyes. As I placed all my new toys back into the bag, I got up to give her a hug. I walked back to my wheelchair because I could feel myself start to bleed from sitting so bent over on her bed. I looked all around the room at my family once again and another tear streamed down my face. Everyone was one step ahead of me with a box of tissues being passed around the room at rapid speed. They were a collective mess, nothing short from the usual.

We all talked for a while and I told everyone about my horrible anesthesia experience.

"The nurse said they took like a big wine size bottle amount of bone marrow from me because they wanted to make sure they had enough. I asked her if they could give back what they don't use cause I need that shit. I'm running low on energy here, can't ya tell."

I coped with my pain by making jokes, but I was seriously feeling lackadaisical. After a couple more stories about the love of my life in the room next to me and the Grey's Anatomy bleeding experience, we called it a day. One of the nurses walked in and told Lex that she just checked the bone marrow bag that they were sending out to get filtered and it was huge. Within two days she would be receiving the harvest. I was positive that day was gonna be a beautiful day to save some lives.

15. ONE MORE TIME

On the ride home, all I saw were stars. Each bump that we went over due to the unpaved roads, hit the not so sweet spots that was just engraved into my back. The moment I walked into my grandmas house I chowed down on my McDonalds chicken nuggets and french fries. After I was fed, I was happy. I was also beginning to see a bit straighter, finally. The nuggets were kicking in and I was feeling fueled but still as immobile as before. I laid on the couch, tummy side down because it was the least painful position to be in. As nighttime rolled around, I helplessly decided that it was best to sleep on my stomach and hoped that I wouldn't toss and turn too much. I normally sleep in about 20 different positions at night so I was praying that tonight wasn't going to be one of those nights. Though, I didn't have much choice if I wanted to be in the least pain possible and not bleed everywhere. I laid flat down in my grandpa's bed and slept with the side of my face squished against a pillow. My dad laid next to me and watched the TV show, Monk. I don't think he slept a wink that night as oppose to how often he slept every other night. His max amounts of sleep were about 2-3 hours anyway, so not much of a change. I woke up at 4am bright eyed and bushy tailed because I felt something dripping onto my sides. I turned, my head over to look at my dad to tell him that I was pretty sure I was bleeding. He got up to check and assured me that blood was trickling out of my bandages. He cleaned up both of my sides before I asked him if he try to stop the bleeding. His reaction was priceless. He looked at me with eyes wide open and asked, "Who? Me?"

"No the guy next door" I said as I rolled my eyes. "Yes, you."

He rolled over to me in the bed and pressed down on my back.

"Am I hurting you?" escaped from his mouth about 20 times within the 10 seconds he was there.

I stayed up for the next few hours until it was time to get ready for school. As 7 am rolled around, I finally managed to get up and throw on my bright pink colored uniform shirt. I changed from one pair of black sweats to another. Thankfully I was able to wear sweatpants and nonuniform shoes for as long as I needed because my tight ass school pants would of definitely disrupted the wound and I was not about to bleed out in the middle of class. As I finished getting poorly dressed, my dad looked at me and said,

"Are you sure you wanna go. You can't even walk right. Do you really wanna sit in pain for hours. You know you're gonna be in trouble if it starts to bleed."

I listened, but respectfully disagreed. I was determined to get my ass to school. Everything that everyone did to ensure that I didn't miss a damn day and here I was about to slack on *them*. However, a few dad looks later and I was choosing the better and probably smarter option even though I didn't admit it at the time. And so, I laid back in bed and fell asleep. There wasn't much to do but sleep. If I stood up and attempted movement, I bled. If I sat down, I bled. Basically if I breathed incorrectly, I bled. Thankfully though, that only lasted another 2 days.

Wednesday was the day that Alexa would receive the bone marrow and thankfully within those two days I was feeling somewhat better. My dad and I visited my mom and Alexa that afternoon and we fortunately made it just in time to see her before she got the infusion. I stared at the bag that was filled to the brim with my bone marrow in complete and utter awe. First of all, I still couldn't even believe that the procedure was done and I was about to *literally* be one with my sister, forever. Second, my jaw was about to hit the damn floor when I saw the *size* of the bag that the marrow was in. I watched the nurse attach the line from the bag into Alexa's IV. I stood next to her bed and held her hand as we followed the flow of red liquid with our eyes. From the bag, into the line, and finally into her arm...

"You're in me. We're one now. Forever. Oh damn, now I'm gonna be as crazy as you." Alexa said as we laughed and teared together. The next couple of days were the most crucial. The hope was that she would respond well to the bone marrow and her platelet count would rise.

There was not much change on the first day. On the second day, Lex acquired a few mouth sores on the insides of her cheeks and around her lips but her counts were still at 0. Her doctor said that normally the patient receiving would get worse before they get better. Once the body began to (hopefully) appropriately react, it would make a home for the new and healthy marrow. The recognition of such event would show by having her counts skyrocket. However, as the days continued to pass, Lex was feeling her lowest of lows. Her mouth and lips were covered in painful sores and blisters which made it almost impossible for her to eat. She tried her absolute best to fuel herself with something each day because she didn't want to have to resort to needed a feeding tube again. Her movements also became less and less available to her each and every day. The worst part, her sly attitude that she was *just* getting back was beginning to fade away again.

As I continued to visit each day, I watched Alexa's appearance change drastically. I knew her doctors said that she would have to get worse first, but seeing all of this happen so quickly was terrifying. The days passed ever so slowly and her counts still didn't move. Nothing started to take and we were all aware of it, though we continued to have faith. My small amount of patience were running thin at this point. This *had* to work because… well it just had too. At the same time though, time was running out. If the bone marrow wasn't accepted within two weeks of the infusion, the time for her body to allow the acceptance was up.

Two weeks passed and the only thing that happened was a moment of delayed excitement. One afternoon, calls were made around the world to rejoice because her counts shot up to 100. However, the hours following the phone calls were full of labored happiness because they had then dropped back down to zero. The heartbreak after being given an inch of happiness was brutal. It all felt like a game at this point and no one wanted to fucking play.

With that, the next and final option was in sight and that was a stem cell transplant. A stem cell transplant was similar to the bone marrow transplant but it was known as the out-patient version. It was basically an immune boost so the already received bone marrow could attach and finally provide what Alexa's body needed. However, the preparation for this transplant was lengthy and quite physically draining. I would have to receive two Neutropenic shots a day for 10 days. The shots would cause my body to rapidly produce white blood cells to the point of overflow. They would then be taken from me to provide for Alexa. The procedure was about the same as being hooked up to a dialysis machine. I would have an IV in both arms, one pulling the blood and having the white blood cells sorted, and the other transporting the newly filtered blood back into me. It sounded pretty scary but time was ticking and it needed to be done. The same night I was told about the procedure was the day that I started the neutropenic shots. The following morning a nurse came to my grandmas house at 7am before I left for school to give me my first out of two shots for the day. I would receive the next one twelve hours later, around the time I went to visit Alexa. I would go to the outpatient center for it and then I was good to go.

The first few days of receiving the shots were effortless. Just a minor pinch in my arm twice a day and all was good. My job was done for the day. I was aware of the joint pains that I may receive because of the amount of white blood cells that were being produced in my body but I was almost positive I wasn't going to get any of those. I'm indestructible, right? As day 6 came along, I began to feel slight aches and pains in my hips but nothing extremely detrimental. On day 7, while talking to my principle at TMLA, I had a shock of pain go through my left leg. The immense agony was quick to occur and slow to leave. I tried to cut our conversation short because if I didn't move within the next few seconds I might of caused a scene in the spot that I was in. I stood up to to give her a hug and felt the pain go right up my spin to the middle of my back. I limped away with as much ease as possible and thought about the fact that I had 4 days left and 8 more shots to endure. Each day the pain became worse. It felt like growing pains, times ten. I swallowed the discomfort as much as possible and reminded myself that I was almost there. Each shot that I was given was one closer to the last and that's all I kept focus on.

The day before my last two shots, I was told what was going to happen for the stem cell. I was gong to have another small procedure to insert a catheter into my neck due to the inability to find my veins. They described it as what I understood as, a small tube that would basically be protruding from my neck. I believed it was as painful as it sounded. And to top it all off, it was all happening on a school day. Since my record was already shot, I figured why even try to maneuver the procedure. Also, Alexa needed this shit done *yesterday,* so now it was!

Tuesday rolled around and I had my final shot in the morning. By 8am, I was already in the pre-opt room dressing in my hospital wear and getting my IV attached to my hand. I was going to be put out again which I'm sure is no secret, but I wasn't very excited for. I met with the anesthesiologist and the doctor who was doing the procedure. Frankly, I was kind of over the talking to just about *everyone*, so I nodded my head and kept it all going. I played with my hospital band and laughed a bunch with my mom before I was up and walking in to the last and final waiting area before being brought to the procedure room. A few swipes on Instagram and I heard my name being called.

As I followed the woman in scrubs, we walked into a room with a ceiling that was as high as my non glasses eyes could see. I felt like I was in that scene in Willy Wonka where the little boy gets shrunk and everything and everyone seems so massive.

"Just lay up on here. And put your head on the neck rest." The nurse said in the sweetest princess voice.

I wasn't phased by the niceness because I was still scared as hell. I just wanted to get all this over with. It seemed like time was slowing down just when I wanted it to speed the fuck up.

I did what I was told…for the first time in forever. I laid down, got as comfortable as possible, and closed my eyes. The next thing I recall was waking up the in the post-opt room. I was in an all white room near the front of the floor and the fact that I knew ny exact location was quite terrifying to me. I was assured that I've been here too often. I looked over my shoulder and saw a man standing next to a big grey machine playing with tiny tubes that I assumed was going to be attached to me within the next couple of minutes. When I set my attention elsewhere, I looked straight and saw my mom. She was looking down at her phone, and while I didn't have my glasses on yet, I swore I saw tears and black eyeliner streaming down her face.

"Can I have my glasses please". I was curious to know if the sniffling was coming from her.

As she placed them on my face and sat back down with her head down, I knew it was her. She then continued her exploration on her phone as she began to shake.

"What happened. Who's texting you?" I asked semi aggressively.

I got no response, just silence and tears. I got up from my chair and walked over to her. The man walked around the chair and practically pulled me down, telling me that I was at fall risk. I didn't listen very well. I took the phone from my mom's hands and read the texts that were displayed on it; it was from my dad.

The doctors just came in. They said they can't do much more for her. They put her back on the oxygen because she was having trouble breathing. They wanna meet with us all to explain to that there's nothing left to do. Finish with Dee and when you come up, we'll all go if she's feeling up to it. I love you. I'm sorry.

I didn't necessarily understand how before I went for the procedure, everything was dandy and now Alexa was literally helpless. She was all ready and prepped to receive the stem cell transplant, life was ready to get back on track and now, this?! So, from the moment I woke up, all hell was breaking loose yet again.

I decided to check all this out for myself. I walked out the door with my mom's phone in hand. The man followed me outside of the room and grabbed my arm, firmly telling me that "I had to sit down". I listened to his stern statement and followed up by showing him the text.

"The doctors wanna see my sisters family and that constitutes me too, so…I gotta go."

I continued to walk down the hallway, walking past the nurses station who were trying to stop me as well. I wasn't quite sure if they didn't understand that I was going to walk off the floor with or without them, but they continued to badger me while I gave them all the same response. They were fairly more agreeable and told me that I had to at least be brought up in a wheelchair because of the whole 'fall risk' thing.

"If you can catch me before I walk out the door then, yeah sure."

As I made it to the double doors, I fell back into a wheelchair that came blazing at the back of my knees. My mom was holding onto the handle for stability while we all managed our way to the elevator. We got in and went right up to the meeting room. I was rolled to the front door by a nurse and transferred to a regular chair immediately. I saw my dad sitting in the corner with his head down, gentle tears washing down his face. My mom walked in behind me and ran out in an instant proclaiming that, 'she couldn't do this again.' Both her and my dad had just been apart of this meeting not too long ago with my grandma. As painful as it was then, this felt like it was going to be ten times worse because it was a child, their child, who had no reason to die due to a prior condition, a life full of happy ahead of her.

It was now up to my dad and I to sit and listen to all the bullshit that was about to come out of everyone's mouths. It wasn't anyones fault, but in the moment I wanted to blame the entire world for not doing more. We were accompanied by just about every doctor Alexa had at Cohens, as well as someone from each team that she was apart of. I sat in my chair and did what my dad did, look at the floor. I remember getting offered tissues by Alexa's social work intern but abruptly declining because there was no way I was going to cry. Why? Besides the fact that I have no emotion, I had no fucking clue what was happening. I was positive that nothing anybody said was going to clear it up. I sat and continued to look around the table full of people telling us that this was her the finish line and unfortunately she wasn't going to be able to cross it.

After this meeting from hell was adjourned, we all walked out of the circle table room and took the elevator up to Alexa's room. This was the first time I was going to see her since I had left her last night. Everything wasn't necessarily okay then, but everything wasn't over. Now, it was over. Time was up, or at least that's what everyone was saying, though I still wanted to see this drastic downfall for myself.

As we all approached her door, one of the nurses on the transplant floor informed us that she was moved to ICU because she was being put on a ventilator after being intubated again.

"What the fuck happened when I was asleep?" I said with a much attitude as one can imagine.

I still couldn't quite wrap my head around all these sudden changes but I didn't have much time to do so. I had to adjust and I had to do so quickly. My dad and I walked hand in hand downstairs to the ICU and made our way to the last room in the back corner of the floor. We walked in the first door and laced ourselves up with gowns, gloves and masks, the usual. We turned the door handle and slowly walked in. I saw my mom rocking back and forth in the corner chair while staring right in the direction of the bed where Alexa laid, lifeless. I couldn't believe what I was seeing. To this day I still can't believe what I saw. It was like the beginning of her diagnosis all over again. She was newly intubated, her skin was as white as snow, and her legs, arms, and feet were filled with water. I didn't know what to think, how to act, or how to feel. Then idea of losing my sister had never crossed my mind. I knew she was fighting to live each day and I knew there was this cancerous poison inside of her, but I never wanted to think of the day that I could quite literally loose her and will have to live a life without her in it. Now, I did and what a lifeless world it was going to be.

I walked over to Alexa's bedside and held her hand. I prayed like I did the first time I saw her intubated. I prayed this wasn't the end. I prayed that something would happen within the next few hours, some miracle just had to occur. I was *sure* that this couldn't be happening but as I continued to pray, I began to realize that maybe something would have happened by itself if she didn't receive the bone marrow. I couldn't help but realize that she only had gotten worse once she received my harvest. And so, I began to blame myself. I stopped praying, continued to hold her hand and thoroughly apologized for what *I* had done. As the tears streamed down my face and fell onto our connected hands, I felt a squeeze. I opened my river filled eyes and watched her squeeze my hand again. I couldn't help but cry even more. I wished I could hear her voice or see her big brown eyes just one last time. I wish we had more time but the clock was ticking and I knew I wasn't the only one who wanted to say goodbye and so I began making *the* phone calls.

My mom started calling her sisters and Alexa's friends while I called my grandpa, nanny, and all of my friends. Within an hour all the calls were made and we sat and waited for everyone to arrive. There was nothing else to do but sit, watch, and wait. That was probably the worst part of it all.

I was so caught up in everything that was happening, I forgot that I had a catheter sticking out of the right side of my neck. I only realized when my dad pointed it out and asked if I was going to get it removed. I genuinely didn't know the answer to that so as I was waiting for the array of family and friends that were likely zooming through the streets to arrive, I asked one of the nurses what to do.

"I'll have someone come downstairs to remove it for you" she said.

"Thank You" I said with the fakest happy smile known to man.

I was anything but happy right now, but everything continued to be unregistering in my mind. Of course I knew that within a few hours my sister would be passed on but I still didn't want to accept that. That happens an awful lot in unexpected deaths and I'll be the first to say that it fucking sucks, but ultimately, it has to be done. It is never easy and it will never get easier to accept the fact that a loved one is gone, but the constant knowledge of having them in your heart and living through their memories helps the grieving process.

I stood outside the room and daydreamed about tomorrow, what it would look like, how I would feel, what the day would consist of. I was awaken from this demonic fantasy when a man walked up to the door and stepped inside the room asking for me.

"Hey. I'm here to remove the catheter."

"Right now? Right here?'

"Yeah we can do it here."

I gave him the largest look of confusion in the world. With that, we walked off to an unoccupied room next to my sisters.

"Wait, is it gonna hurt?"

"It's not gonna hurt. It's just gonna feel weird. That's what patients tell me all the time. It feels like an out body experience, I guess. I don't know how to explain it" he said, followed by a laugh to ensure that I would be "just fine".

I waved my dad over because I wanted him to come inside and hold my hand. This thing that was inserted into my neck was about to be pulled out by this nicely dressed and insanely good smelling, mans' hands. I sat on the bed, closed my eyes and squeezed my dad's hand for dear life. I felt a little tug on my neck and heard a loud pop near my ear and the damage was done. I got up and wiped the drying tears from my eyes.

"See it wasn't so bad? It just felt weird, right?"

I nodded and smiled. He handed me an ice pack to put on my neck because of the soreness and swelling that was going to occur within the next few hours. As I waked out of the room cradling the ice pack, I watched 10 people sprint down the hall and up to my dad and I. My sisters childhood best friend Theresa Shields was one fo the first people to show up. Following her was Alexa's high school best friends Kailey Halpin, Caitlin Kessel, and Isabella Spallino. Carly and her mom was next, accompanied by Geresa and her entire family as well as my middle school best friend Sabino Ciociari and his sister. The people continued to flow in. Within two hours of getting the word out, the room was filled with our loved ones. The tears falling from everyones eyes could fill a swimming pool. The energy in the room was nothing short of absolutely and utterly sorrowful.

When the clock hit around 10, one of the doctors on the floor walked into the room. All heads turned his way. He asked to speak to my mom, dad, and I privately and so we all walked outside together. With muttered words that I didn't pay any mind too, all I heard was, "we can either leave her on the ventilator or remove the tube and let her breath on her own for however long possible." Both options fucking sucked because both of them meant death. One sounded more painful than the other. After months of her suffering on the daily, we ultimately decided to remove the tube, allowing her to say goodbye when she was ready. As we walked back in, Geresas dad, Jerry, asked if he could speak. Jerry was known for his wise words of wisdom and he always knew what to say in any situation. He sent Alexa off with prayers and words that no one in that room will ever forget. The flow of emotions continued all throughout his sermon. As it was coming to an end, Sesa, my mom, and I circled around Lex's bed and continued to bawl. We all waited for the doctor to come back into the room to remove the tube. As we waited, my mom grabbed my sisters hand and told her what was about to happen.

"Mama, we're going to remove the tube, okay? You don't have to suffer anymore. Okay?"

The following event is one that haunts me to his day. As my mom said this, Alexa's body jumped. I felt like that took whatever was left in her soul. My head dropped to the floor because all I could imagine was that being is a solid scream saying, "NO! I can do this!" I will forever replay that scene in my head because I wish it would have ended, in any other way than this one. The night was for sure going to be a reoccurring nightmare.

A few minutes after 10:30 pm the doctor strolled in with two nurses at his side. We all stood, watched and cried as he gently pulled the tube from Alexa's mouth. He raised his hand to look at his watch as his other hand held the stethoscope on her heart. One beat. Two beats. Three beats. A final breath.

16. FOREVER AFTER ALL

Now we had one more angel watching over and blessing our every move. How do you walk away from someone so easily? Does the pain ever really go away? I'd like to say that within a few days I was able to pick up life like nothing happened, but reality was, my life was forever shifted.

I knew I had to step up to somewhat patch up this broken family. There was barely a word spoken in my grandmas house the days following her passing. The only noise that occurred was the appointment making for a meeting at the funeral home. All the silence made my mind run wild and I couldn't bear it much longer. When I got to the point of explosion, I ran out of the house in a panic and walked right to my car. Sesa followed me and asked where I was going.

"I can't stay in there anymore. I'm gonna go crazy."

"Where are ya gonna go?"

"I'm just gonna drive around for a bit"

"I'll come with ya?" And off we went riding around the streets, no intention of going anywhere.

The road managed to take me to TMLA. I left Sesa in the car to ponder her thoughts while I walked down the hill towards the Wexford Terrace entrance. I rang the bell and when asked "who is it?" I said "Deanna" and was buzzed in immediately. I knew that the news spread like rapid fire. I didn't even contact anyone other than my closest friends and family to come to the hospital the night prior, but I was positive that the entire world was one step ahead of me. As I walked up the stairs, I was pensive about seeing everyone, but at the same time I needed to talk. I never stop talking and being home and inaudible was not allowing me to grieve in my own ways. I knew the one place that I could be myself was at my second home. After getting to the top of the stairs, I headed straight to my principal, Mrs. Cordes. She hugged me and asked me why in the heck I was there.

"I really didn't wanna be home right now."

She nodded and consoled me as we sat down and talked for a bit. Ten minutes into our conversation, the phone rang. It was a call from the guidance office.

"Ms. Moore says there's a couple girls downstairs, is it okay if I tell them to come up?"

"Yeah of course" I said with a smile.

I had no idea what I agreed to or who was even down there but I would know in a few seconds. I wiped my tiny tears with a tissue and heard a knock on the door. Mrs. Cordes opened the door and in came three sobbing fools, my friends. Carly, Bella, and Layla strolled in and I graciously handed them the box of tissues that was in my lap. They all embraced me in a hug and continued our mini intervention in the office. When the bell rang to switch classes, we got up and went our separate ways. The girls went to their next period class and I wandered around the halls for a while. When I saw my teachers and friends in the hallways, they all ran up to give me hugs and kisses. Besides the immense love I was receiving, the vibe in the building was somber as ever. It wasn't the normal 'TMLA vibe'. The halls felt dark, the girls were quiet, the lessons were barely being taught in classes. Many teachers didn't even have a full class that day because everyone was so terribly upset about Alexa's passing. It genuinely affected *everyone* and I was seeing it first freakin hand. It was wild. The tears streaming down the teachers faces when they saw mine, watching my friends sit in class and do nothing but cry, it was nothing short of the most abnormal day at TMLA.

I left before the next bell rang and walked up the hill to get back to my car. I waved at Sesa through the rear view mirror and watched her wipe her tears on her sleeve. I felt a bit better after our therapy session but I still didn't want to go home though. I had a lot of work to do in the next couple of days. The meeting with the people from the funeral home was the following day, and I had to do all the photo boards for the wake and write a eulogy for the mass as soon as possible. I figured I was going to be taking the lead with all the arrangements for the wake so I had to make sure to plan everything else accordingly so I had enough time for everything. My next stop was to CVS to print out the hundreds of photos I collected of Alexa and our entire family the night before. Then, I was off to Michaels to buy stickers and poster boards to display all of our memories for everyone to admire at the wake. My whole day consisted of cutting up photos, having double sided tape attached to every surface in my view and stickers flying all around the house.

When I got home, I brought in my hundreds of dollars worth of arts and crafts and got to work. I made 8 poster board collages within the three days that I had before the first viewing. My whole family gathered at Gleason's funeral home at once to see Alexa lay peacefully before she was going to be seen by the other several hundreds of our loved ones. I walked my grandpa and nanny up to the casket first. My mom and dad followed behind us and my aunt and cousins behind them. Within the first couple minutes of the afternoon viewing, people were flooding into the room to say their farewells. I felt like I was having deja vu, having just done this for my grandma but now, it was my sister.

Never would I have imagined that this day would have come so soon. I didn't cry for both days of the viewing because I was so incredibly numb the entire time. The morning following the second viewing was the funeral day. At around 2am I finally found some form of inspiration to write a eulogy. I was as prepared as one could be for this day to occur. I felt like I had everything ready for the mass and just about enough mental and emotional stability to endure the next few hours.

All of my immediate family arrived at the funeral home to send Alexa off before they closed her casket for good. We then loaded into the limo and our respective cars and headed to St. Mel's Church for the mass. If I told you what happened that day it would have inquired a whirlwind of question marks after each statement because I'm not quite sure what went on. All I remember was reading these 2am words…

So, for anyone and everyone that knew Alexa, y'all knew that she got as far as she did because of the love all of you gave her. So instead of this eulogy being reasons why everyone loved her, we're gonna talk about why she loved everyone. She was a daughter, a sister, a granddaughter, a niece, a cousin, a goddaughter, a best friend, a student, a patient… and the list goes on and on. The first, a daughter to the utmost determined and willing parents that this earth graced us with. Mom and Dad, Alexa couldn't thank you enough for absolutely everything you've ever done for not only her, but for us. If only she could show you the amount of love she has for the both of you, she'd give you the world times ten. Mom, you are the epitome of strong. When Alexa started fighting this battle, you stayed by her side through everything. You and Alexa were practically attached to the hip until her very last day. When I called your phone wanting to talk to you, Alexa would answer. When I called Alexa's phone, wanting to talk to Alexa, she would answer... and then hang up on me. She was and is forever grateful for you sticking by her side through her most difficult life journey in her short lived 20 years. Dad, Alexa is and will always be daddy's little girl. The way she looked up to you and actually looked like you is kinda scary. When Alexa first lost her hair, her immediate response wasn't to cry or feel sorry for herself. Instead, she said, "Now I look even more like daddy". Although Alexa didn't say much when it came to being emotional, she loved and will continue to love and honor both of you everyday. A sister, my department. A lot of people may already know this but I was and will forever be classified as "Alexa's sister". Although I act like I hate it, it truly is the most honorable title I will ever receive. Being 'Alexa's sister' is the best. She was a constant support system. Whenever I was upset, sad, angry, or annoyed, she was there whether I wanted her to be or not. When Alexa first got diagnosed, I couldn't fathom the idea that my best friend was literally fighting for her life. Through surgeries, chemo, radiation, and transplants, Alexa did everything with a smile on her face because she knew her family was waiting behind her. There was no stopping her fight. My biggest fear going into this fight with her was loosing her. Without Alexa, I literally know nothing. She was my brains. So much that in her last month with us, she was filling out my common application in the hospital resource center in between her radiation treatments to ensure that I get into college and make my best attempt to be successful. What a constant blessing it was to not only be in her presence everyday but also have the privilege and honor to call her not only my best friend and movie buddy, but my sister. Being a granddaughter was one of Alexa's finest titles. Growing up under the support of Grandma, may she rest in peace, and Grandpa, was something that the both of us can vouch for being the greatest experiences ever. Both of them shaped her into the person she was and everyone here can vouch for them doing a beyond exceptional job.Whether you were an aunt, uncle or cousin, Alexa influenced everyones lives because of all of you. Guiding her through this journey of life and being loved unconditionally was a quality that all of you aunts and uncles possess. Even though she would roll her eyes for the over affection sometimes, her love was still there and you knew it because she would do such a thing.

Her cousins, close or distant, wether she saw you every day or once a year. No matter who she encountered, you could feel her love through her smile. She appreciated every single one of you like you wouldn't know. A goddaughter to two of her favorite people ever, Uncle Joe and Sesa. Both of you loved her like no other. Your constant love and support for everything and anything that Alexa wanted to pursue in life is incredible. That kind of support is something that not a lot of people can say they experience in a lifetime but you both had her back through everything. Alexa was privileged enough to have encountered so many people that she was able to call her friends and even best friends throughout her time on earth. From her St. Mels family, to TMLA and even her short time at Maritime. Alexa not only impacted hundreds with her presence and beautiful smile, but you all impacted her with your grace and humility. Whether you passed her in the hallways and waved, smiled at her while switching classes or were practically hand in hand wherever you went, you helped her manage to get through elementary school, high school and attempt to take on the 'real world' at college. Alexa had so much love and respect for all of you. Lastly, to everyone that taught, aided, or just genuinely loved and cared for her. Alexa owes all of her intelligence to anyone that gave her any sort of knowledge throughout her life. She owes her graciousness and respect to all those that continued to help her, be not only her nurse but her friend and guide her through her difficult battle. Alexa has so much love for everyone in this room. Her heart was too big for this world and that's why God had to take her so soon. She was so blessed to have each and every one of you inspiring people in her life and she will forever hold these titles close to her heart. And now, for her last and final title, the newest addition, a guardian angel. Alexa may you watch over and guide us all through life and rest with all the angels in Heaven. You were clearly too good for this world. A real life angel on Earth.

...and even that's kind of fuzzy. I remember seeing the whole Church full of our family and friends, new and old, some of our TMLA teachers and sisters, our St. Mel's teachers, recent and not, and so many more. TMLA even sent out a bus to bring girls that wanted to attend Alexa's mass. There was basically only standing room available. As the mass concluded, I walked out the doors and stood on the steps next to our two priests, Father Sauer and Father Lee. I hugged about each and every person that was present in the Church that morning. I then made my way back to the limo to accompany nanny, my grandpa, Chris, Nicky, and our other cousin

Cesar. We were soon going to be following the hearse that was going to take Alexa to pass by my grandmas house and our house one last time. Our final stop was Pinelawn Memorial Cemetery. Recalling any other memory from that day is nearly impossible. Frankly, all I slightly remember is placing white roses on top of her casket before watching her be placed into the mausoleum wall. Days and days passed after Alexa had been gone and every day felt like it was slowly becoming more and more empty. I tried to fill up the void with school and friends, but as everyone else broke down and continued to grieve, I was the one who felt the need to stay strong. If I broke down, who was going to hold us together? So I decided to live out each moment I had through my sister, as if she was still here. I continued putting my college applications through and finally figured out what my top choice was. In May of 2019, I attended my prom with my friends and had the night of my life. I made my sister promise me that she would attend her prom and so when I told her I didn't want to go because, "its not really my thing" which was a straight up lie, I had to promise her I would. In reality, I didn't want to leave her side for a night out. But now I knew she would be looking over me the whole time, so I had to go. The following month, I graduated high school. While I did not receive perfect attendance like I once wished, I received an award that meant more to me than words can describe. I received the Principals Award followed by a standing ovation from everyone in the Queens College auditorium. Normally after receiving awards the only people that are allowed to meet you at the stage stairs are TMLA alumnae from prior years. However, without a sister to walk into the arms of, my two other alumnae sisters greeted me. I walked into the arms of Kailey and Caitlin and couldn't help but shed a few tears. The blessings continued from then on because I also left with an art and service award accompanied by a blue chord. That summer was one I will never forget. We finally had another family vacation to Disney. My Mom, Dad, Soraya, Val Dayanara, Sesa, Chris, Nicky, Omar, and I, all spent 5 days together in the most magical place on earth. The memories we made were ones that will last a lifetime. The end of the month consisted of a new chapter for me, college at Marymount Manhattan. Life was rough now that I was a college gal but I tried to stay as focused as possible because I knew I wouldn't have gotten here without my sister, so I couldn't let her down. Being 'college busy' managed to make the months fly by. As the middle of September rolled around, my family, friends and I were all getting ready to participate in the annual Walk n' Roll hosted by Children's Specialized, the hospital Alexa was cared for in New Brunswick, New Jersey. A bunch of Alexa's nurses were all walking in honor of her.

They even set up a team called "Once Upon a Team" and made shirts for everyone who signed up to walk with us. All teams came together to raise funds and participate as well honor our forever loved ones. The turn out for the event was absolutely incredible and a day I will never forget.

However, within the blink of an eye it was already November. Alexa's one year was approaching ever so quickly. How did I manage to make it 365 days without her? Two years later and I still don't know how I'm somehow surviving. However, I was determined to make her every year in Heaven a special one. It seems like it should be frowned upon or at least joined by some form of sadness but I wanted to rejoice in her love and memories. So, I decided to give back, like she always wanted to do. I decided to partner with Make-A-Wish to donate money that I raised in Alexa's honor. My aunts and I also decided to continue spreading the Christmas spirit by donating toys to the children who were struggling with sicknesses similar to Lex. We got in contact with RWJ and Children's Specialized and made the dream a reality. We purchased some of Alexa's favorite games that made her smile during her rough times in the hospital, wrapped them, and labeled them in her honor. The feeling I received when I gave the presents over to one of the nurses that was assisting us, is a feeling that I wish I could encapsulate for the rest of my life. The abundance of joy and the smile on my face showed it all. All of the experiences and stories that I have acquired throughout my time with my sister and the time without my sister has led me to where I am today, memorializing her name for life with a book about our journey. Alexa taught me a whole bunch during her time on this earth, but she left out one lesson, maybe the most important, how to live in a world without her. Maybe if I had just five more minutes.

CPSIA information can be obtained
at www.ICGtesting.com
Printed in the USA
LVHW010326011021
699202LV00003B/255